CONSIDERABLE PASSIONS

GOLF, THE MASTERS, AND THE LEGACY OF BOBBY JONES

CONSIDERABLE PASSIONS

GOLF, THE MASTERS, AND THE LEGACY OF BOBBY JONES

Featuring Historical Images from Select Private Collections

CATHERINE M. LEWIS

TRIUMPH
BOOKS
CHICAGO

ATLANTA
HISTORY
CENTER

This book is based in part on the Atlanta History Center exhibition, *Down the Fairway with Bobby Jones*.

This book is available in quantity at special discounts for your group or organization.
For further information, contact:

Triumph Books
601 South LaSalle Street
Suite 500
Chicago, Illinois 60605
(312) 939-3330
Fax (312) 663-3557

Printed in the United States.

ISBN 1-57243-354-X

Book and jacket design by Eileen Wagner.

Front cover: © Historic Golf Prints/Ron Watts Collection.

CONTENTS

ACKNOWLEDGEMENTS

Considerable Passions attempts to preserve *Down the Fairway with Bobby Jones*, an exhibition on Jones and the history of golf that opened at the Atlanta History Center in April 1999. The largest permanent exhibition on Jones's life, the project does more than simply recount the details of his biography, which has been adeptly done by journalists, collectors, and golf enthusiasts. Instead, it contextualizes his career within the broader changes in American sport of the twentieth century. To this end, this book, like the exhibition before it, examines the formation of golf clubs and courses, the rise of amateur athletics, and the democratization of the game after World War II. It introduces readers to many players, some of whom achieved stunning victories, and some of whom changed the way the game is played.

Books are always collaborative endeavors that require assistance and guidance; as a result, there are many people to thank. First and foremost is Kimberly Blass, the book's editor. She helped develop the themes, select the photographs, and refine the text. Her commitment to and enthusiasm for the project made it possible. I would also like to thank the executive committee of *Down the Fairway with Bobby Jones*: John P. Imlay Jr., Linton Hopkins, Gene McClure, Sidney L. Matthew, Charles R. Yates, and the late Eugene T. Branch. All experts on Mr. Jones, they contributed stories, insights, and ideas for this volume. Sidney Matthew and his assistants Gwynne Chasom and Cindy Thompson deserve special recognition for their contributions during the production phase. William F. Hull, the History Center's staff photographer, worked tirelessly to ensure that the photographs included in *Considerable Passions* are of the highest quality, all while working on several equally time-consuming projects. A variety of librarians, archivists, and museum professionals helped locate original photographs, including Michael Rose, Eilean Stiener, Anne Salter, Yen Tang, Helen Matthews, and Susan Illis of the Atlanta History Center; Kathy Shoemaker of the Special Collections Department, Robert W. Woodruff Library, Emory University; Daniel O. Cox of the Marietta Museum of History; Mary Civille of the *Atlanta Journal-Constitution*;

Maxine Vigliatta of the United States Golf Association; and the staff of St. Andrews University Library, Scotland. Marty Elgison of Alston & Bird and the family of Robert Tyre Jones Jr. offered enthusiastic support and located images that have rarely been seen. Mike Waldron of the Georgia State Golf Association, Donna Hand of the Atlanta Athletic Club, David Boyd and Danny Yates of Peachtree Golf Club, Glenn Greenspan of Augusta National Golf Club, Thomas Cousins of East Lake Golf Club, Sir Michael Bonnalack of the Royal and Ancient Golf Club of St. Andrews, and the staff of the East Lake Community Foundation also deserve a special thanks.

A variety of golfers and their families helped make this book possible, including: Sandy Carwardine; Louise Suggs; Dorothy Kirby; Charlie Yates; the family of O. B. Keeler; Jane Gunn; the family of Alfred "Tup," Dr. Hamilton, and Oliver Wendell Holmes; the family of George, Harold, and Jack Sargent; Delores Ann Yancey; Tommy Barnes; Charles T. Bell; Aimee Daniel McNeal; Eileen Stulb; and Barrie Naismith Jeffcoat.

The History Center would also like to thank Heidi Hill and Mitch Rogatz at Triumph Books for their willingness to embark on this project. I would like to extend my appreciation to Dr. Rick Beard, Atlanta History Center Executive Director, and Dr. James Southerland, Humanities Department Chair, Brenau University, for encouraging and supporting my research efforts. I would also like to thank Dr. Andy Ambrose, Deputy Director of the Atlanta History Center, for his advice and encouragement throughout this process. Finally, I would like to thank Jonathan Glick, who has come to accept that Mr. Jones is the other man in my life.

Catherine M. Lewis, Ph.D.

Curator, Down the Fairway with Bobby Jones

Atlanta History Center

Assistant Professor of English and History

Brenau University

REMEMBERING BOBBY JONES

Bob Jones's family moved to the Atlanta suburb of East Lake when he was seven. His parents, Robert and Clara, bought a house next to the Atlanta Athletic Club's East Lake Golf Course hoping that the fresh air would improve their son's fragile health. It did, and Bob took to following Stewart Maiden, the Scottish pro at the club, around the golf course. Bob proved to be a natural athlete, and by the tender age of fourteen he had qualified to play in his first national championship, the U.S. Amateur.

As a teenager, Bob was a determined and aggressive competitor who often lost his temper. The nadir of this habit came when he disqualified himself from the British Open in 1921. What a great story it is that he conquered his frustration and anger and became the epitome of all that a sportsman should be.

It was my good fortune that our family moved alongside the fourth hole at East Lake in 1917 when I was four years old. I slipped across the fence onto the course to watch Bob, who was just beginning his competitive career. He was always kind to me; he even introduced me to that great elixir of Atlanta—Coca-Cola. We remained lifelong friends, and I watched his tournaments with great interest. He retired just as I was beginning my own career, and I always benefited from his kindness and support.

I was blessed to have known Bob as long as I did. From the early 1930s through the 1940s, we played many friendly rounds of golf together. Even after his retirement, he was an unmatched competitor. I cherish my memories of things he said to me, particularly in 1925 after he lost the U.S. Open by a single stroke. When he returned to East Lake, I told him that I was sorry he lost. He replied, "Don't worry about it son, you never really know who your friends are until you lose."

In 1948, Bob was diagnosed with a neurological problem that finally caused a complete degeneration of the spinal cord and forced him to give up the game he loved. He was always brave and gracious in the face of this extreme pain. When friends and strangers expressed their sympathy, he often replied, "Just remember, you always play the ball where it lies." That was the kind of man he was.

My admiration for Bob is endless, and I am delighted to have been involved in helping to preserve his legacy through *Down the Fairway with Bobby Jones*, a permanent exhibition on Bob and golf in Georgia at the Atlanta History Center. I am also pleased to be involved in helping to bring this companion volume to life. They are both fine testaments to the life and legacy of this great man.

Charles R. Yates

1938 British Amateur Champion

Secretary, Augusta National Golf Club

Bobby Jones with Charlie Yates
Charles R. Yates

Bobby Jones
Jones Family

A TRUE RENAISSANCE MAN

In this era of specialization, our lives are valued more for a particular talent than for the universality we can demonstrate in a wide variety of areas. But Bobby Jones, who came upon the sporting scene in the Roaring Twenties, was a true Renaissance man—a concept that is all but lost today.

Jones was a hero as a human being as well as a hero as a sports figure. Divine providence and a superior intellect worked together to make it so. He was more than just the greatest golfer of his era; he had more ambition than that and other things to accomplish. Imagine Mozart being a part-time symphony writer or Picasso painting just as a hobby. Now, imagine someone like Bobby Jones, who reached the pinnacle of perfection in his sport all while pursuing other noteworthy endeavors.

For these reasons, the legacy of Bob Jones comprises much more than his sporting achievements. No one ever conceived of the Grand Slam before Jones dreamed up the notion in 1926. And when Jones achieved that goal, he moved on to other equally marvelous feats created by his fertile genius.

Considerable Passions, the companion volume to *Down the Fairway with Bobby Jones*, a permanent exhibition at the Atlanta History Center, is a tribute to Bob Jones's life and the way he lived it. But it goes further than simply recounting the details of his biography; it examines how he influenced golf and the subsequent changes that made it a more democratic game.

Jones was an ordinary man in some important ways. He was a family man and a lawyer who, when his workday week was complete, played golf for recreation. But the key to understanding Jones is to understand his priorities. They were God, family, occupation, and, lastly, golf.

Jones was able to retire from competitive golf at age twenty-eight because he was secure in these priorities. Other champion sportsmen, such as Muhammad Ali, Michael Jordan, and George Foreman, all returned after retirement to reprise their sporting prowess, long after the sun had set on their best performances. Perhaps it was because sports had become the top priority in their lives and their main reason for living. Perhaps they were not confident that their sporting record was sufficient in itself to speak to future generations. And perhaps these and other champions returned to the arena for money. But Jones did not suffer from such insecurity, and he did not need a huge purse to summon his competitive passion. For Jones, there was ample reward simply in doing one's best.

Jones carried this penchant for excellence in other areas of his life, too. After his retirement in 1930, he sought to help the common man elevate his understanding and enjoyment of the game of golf. The *How I Play Golf* series was so expertly produced by Warner Brothers that even today it is the standard by which all other instructional films are measured. Jones also wanted to express himself in helping to create the zenith of golf courses—Augusta National. This course serves as a true Jones memorial in that it incorporates his notions of beauty and balance in sports and nature.

This book is appropriate for another reason. It demonstrates the love that the innately shy Jones expressed to other people, but also the way others responded in kind. It reveals the importance of one's character. When enjoying trips to his adopted homeland of Scotland, Jones remarked: "It was a wonderful experience to go about a town where people wave at you from doorways and windows, where strangers smile at you and greet you by name, often your first name." Fondly called "Our Bobby" by the Scots, Jones was always "one of us."

Jones's life has much for us to appreciate, even today. As did Bob Jones, we can all aspire to be heroes in our everyday lives, although we may never realize the impact we have had. Once, when presented with a manuscript recounting the Grand Slam, Jones read the glowing account of his achievement. In response, he penned a letter to its author, stating, "I only wish I had been that good." But you were, Mr. Jones, you certainly were.

Sidney L. Matthew,
Author, *The Life and Times of Bobby Jones*

Brewerton Cartoon Collection (MSS-241), Atlanta History Center

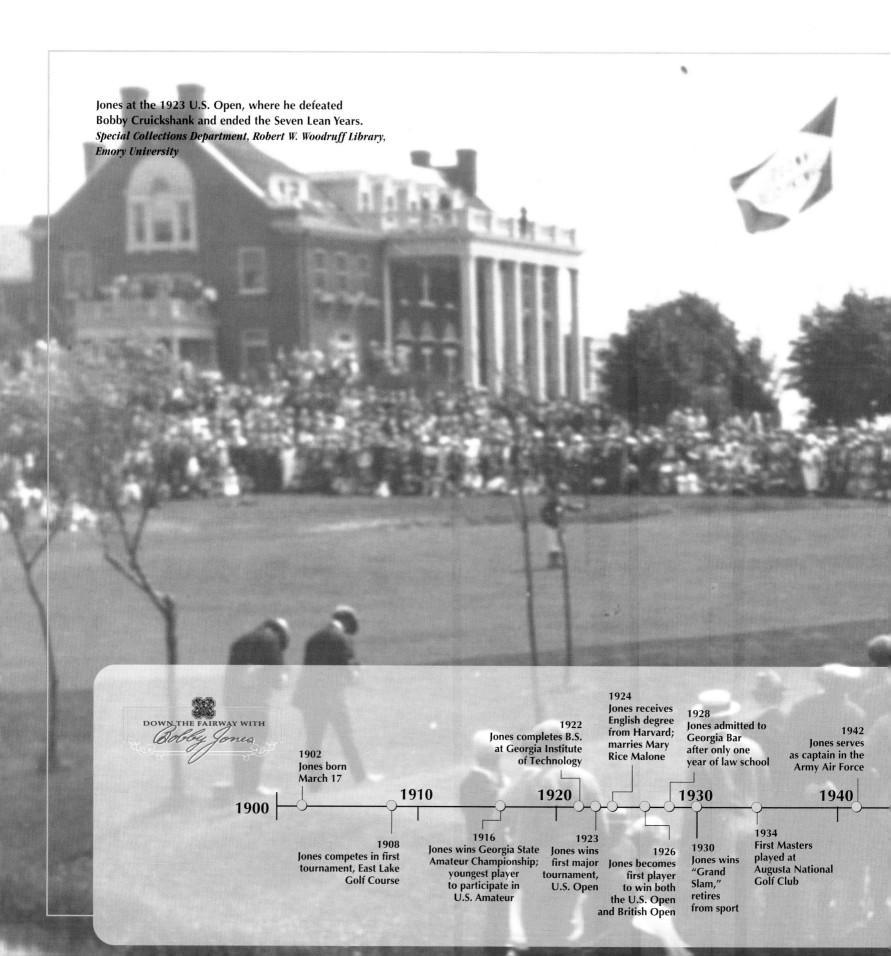

Jones at the 1923 U.S. Open, where he defeated
Bobby Cruickshank and ended the Seven Lean Years.
*Special Collections Department, Robert W. Woodruff Library,
Emory University*

DOWN THE FAIRWAY WITH
Bobby Jones

1902
Jones born
March 17

1922
Jones completes B.S.
at Georgia Institute
of Technology

1924
Jones receives
English degree
from Harvard;
marries Mary
Rice Malone

1928
Jones admitted to
Georgia Bar
after only one
year of law school

1942
Jones serves
as captain in the
Army Air Force

1900   **1910**   **1920**   **1930**   **1940**

1908
Jones competes in first
tournament, East Lake
Golf Course

1916
Jones wins Georgia State
Amateur Championship;
youngest player
to participate in
U.S. Amateur

1923
Jones wins
first major
tournament,
U.S. Open

1926
Jones becomes
first player
to win both
the U.S. Open
and British Open

1930
Jones wins
"Grand
Slam,"
retires
from sport

1934
First Masters
played at
Augusta National
Golf Club

PLAY THE BALL WHERE IT LIES

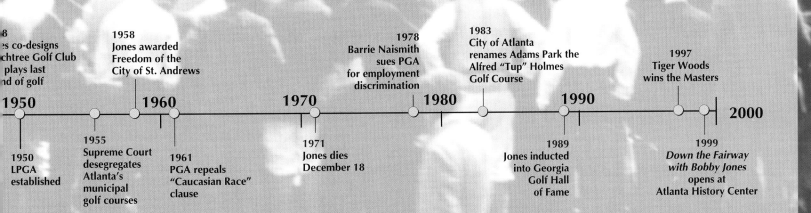

1958
es co-designs
chtree Golf Club
plays last
nd of golf

1958
Jones awarded
Freedom of the
City of St. Andrews

1978
Barrie Naismith
sues PGA
for employment
discrimination

1983
City of Atlanta
renames Adams Park the
Alfred "Tup" Holmes
Golf Course

1997
Tiger Woods
wins the Masters

1950   **1960**   **1970**   **1980**   **1990**   **2000**

1950
LPGA
established

1955
Supreme Court
desegregates
Atlanta's
municipal
golf courses

1961
PGA repeals
"Caucasian Race"
clause

1971
Jones dies
December 18

1989
Jones inducted
into Georgia
Golf Hall
of Fame

1999
*Down the Fairway
with Bobby Jones*
opens at
Atlanta History Center

"When one plays against Mr. Jones, he has only the pleasure of being defeated by the greatest of all golfers and the finest of all sportsmen." **T. PHILIP PERKINS**

He was the most famous and best-loved athlete of the 1920s and 1930s. He bridged the early and modern periods of American golf and helped promote and popularize the game on an international stage. He established his home state of Georgia as the nation's golfing capital, while his sportsmanship called singular attention to the game's best traditions. He was Robert Tyre "Bobby" Jones Jr., and he has left the world of golf an enduring legacy.

Jones's successes on and off the golf course have inspired generations of men and women of all ages, backgrounds, and races to take up the game. No other player, not even Tiger Woods, has had a greater impact on the way golf is played. The integrity of Jones's game and life continue to be the standard by which all other athletes are measured. In an era of million-dollar contracts and labor disputes, Jones remains a role model worthy of respect and emulation. He was, as Jones biographer Sidney L. Matthew contends, a "hero after 5 o'clock."

Bobby Jones was born on March 17, 1902, in Atlanta's Grant Park neighborhood, just as golf was becoming popular in the United States. While golf had made its first appearance on the American scene during the nation's early years, at private institutions such as the South Carolina Golf Club (1786) and the Savannah Golf Club (ca. 1794), in the late nineteenth and early twentieth centuries horse racing, baseball, lawn tennis, cycling, and prize fighting held much greater appeal for the masses. But between 1854 and 1895, more than 125 golf clubs were established in the United States. Half a dozen of these were located in Georgia, including the Capital City Club (1883), Glen Arven Country Club (1892), Brookwood Links (1898), Atlanta Athletic Club (1898), and Augusta Country Club (1899). The United States Golf Association was founded in 1894 and the first U.S. Amateur tournament was held that same year. Golf was growing in popularity and visibility. So it was perhaps fitting that in the year Jones was born, Coburn Haskell patented the rubber core ball—two events that together helped to usher in the modern era of golf.

With the creation of a more durable ball and the mass production and standardization of iron clubs, many

Americans, including Jones's parents, Robert and Clara, became avid golfers. So that they could further enjoy their newfound sport, in the summer of 1907 the Joneses decided to rent a house overlooking the second fairway of the Atlanta Athletic Club's new East Lake Golf Course, at the east end of Atlanta's trolley line.

The next summer, the Jones family moved permanently to East Lake. Jones's parents took lessons from the club's Scottish golf professional, Jimmy Maiden, before he left to become the pro at the Nassau Country Club on Long Island, New York. Soon Maiden's younger brother, Stewart, became the club pro. According to Jones, it "was the luckiest thing that ever happened to me in golf." (Jimmy Maiden, though, remained involved in Jones's career. On the eve of the 1923 U.S. Open, Jimmy gave Jones the now-famous Calamity Jane, a putter made by Robert Condie that Maiden brought with him from Carnoustie, Scotland.) Young Bobby took to following the Scotsman around the course. After watching Stewart play, although with no formal lessons, he would "get a cup full of old balls . . . and go out to the thirteenth green and pitch them all on and putt them out." He soon developed his love for the game, even once asking his father, "What do people do on Sundays who don't play golf?"

At age eleven, Jones shot an 80 at East Lake. Two years later, he defeated Archer Davidson at Druid Hills Golf Club and broke the course record with a 73. At age fourteen, as a freshman at Atlanta's Tech High School, Jones won the Georgia State Amateur Championship at Capital City Club, defeating his childhood friend and fellow Atlanta Athletic Club member Perry Adair. This win qualified Jones as the youngest competitor in the U.S. Amateur, played at the Merion Cricket Club near Philadelphia. Although the "new kid from Dixie" lost to reigning amateur champion Robert A. Gardner in the third round, Jones's competitive golfing career had begun.

In 1915, the members of the Atlanta Athletic Club presented "Our Little Bob" with this pocket watch after he won the club championships at both the Athletic Club and the Druid Hills Golf Club. *1995.14.M5, Atlanta History Center; William F. Hull, photographer*

From 1916 to 1922, Jones played in dozens of tournaments, but did not capture a national title—largely because he was unable to control his temper. In his autobiography, Jones recalls that " . . . I never won a major championship until I learned to play golf against something, and not someone. And that something was par . . . It took me many years to learn that, and a great deal of heartache." Sportswriter O. B. Keeler, Jones's close friend, termed this period "The Seven Lean Years." The low point came at the 1921 British Open at St. Andrews when Jones picked up his ball on the eleventh hole and disqualified himself. Later that summer, he injured a spectator by throwing a club during the U.S. Amateur. Jones used these "inglorious failures" to transform his attitude and his game, declaring, "I never learned anything from a match that I won."

While studying at Harvard, a more mature Jones beat Bobby Cruickshank in the playoffs at the 1923 U.S. Open at Inwood Country Club in New York, thus ending the lean years. From 1923 to 1930, Jones won thirteen major tournaments—five U.S. Amateurs (1924, 1925, 1927, 1928, and 1930), four U.S. Opens (1923, 1926, 1929, and 1930), three British Opens (1926,

The gold key to the city was a "symbol of affection of his friends and neighbors." *1995.90.M1, Atlanta History Center; William F. Hull, photographer*

1927, and 1930), and one British Amateur (1930). Keeler termed this series of victories "The Seven Fat Years." In 1926, Jones became the first American golfer to win the "double"—the U.S. Open and British Open—and was rewarded with a ticker-tape parade in New York City. It

would be six years before another player—Gene Sarazen—would match this feat.

In 1927, Jones returned to St. Andrews. The last time he played the Scottish course he withdrew from the competition in despair; this time he walked onto the course a mature competitor, with degrees in mechanical engineering from the Georgia Institute of Technology and English literature from Harvard University. He had also married Atlanta's Mary Rice Malone, and had one daughter, Clara (he would eventually have a son, Robert Tyre III, and another daughter, Mary Ellen). Jones continued to play in golf tournaments while attending Emory University Law School in Atlanta. Halfway through his second year, he took the bar exam, passed, and joined his father's law firm, Jones, Evins, Moore & Powers (now Alston & Bird).

But Jones's greatest accomplishment came in 1930 when he became the first and only golfer to win the Grand Slam—the British Amateur, British Open, U.S. Open, and U.S. Amateur. The lawyer and amateur golfer began the year by winning the Southeastern Open in Augusta. He then traveled to the Royal St. George's Golf Club in Sandwich, England, to captain the victorious Walker Cup team and to play in an exhibition match in Oxhey. Next it was on to his favorite course, St. Andrews, for the British Amateur—the only major tournament Jones had not won, but the one he soon would call "the most important tournament of my life." Before a gallery of twenty thousand fans, he won seven straight eighteen-hole matches and defeated Roger H. Wethered in the final thirty-six-hole match, 7 to 6. Astonished by Jones's performance, one spectator joked, "They ought to burn him at the stake. He's a witch."

After a brief holiday in Paris, Jones traveled to the Royal Liverpool Golf Club in Hoylake for the British Open (June 18–20) and defeated Macdonald Smith and Leo Diegel by two strokes. *The Times* in London declared it a "triumph of courage and of putting." After becoming the first golfer in forty years and the first American golfer to win both British tournaments in a single year, New York rewarded Jones with a second ticker-tape parade up Broadway. (Jones was the only person ever given two ticker-tape parades in New York, until astronaut John Glenn received his second in 1998.)

Two weeks later (July 10–12), Jones won the U.S. Open at Interlachen Country Club in Minnesota during a stifling heat wave. On the ninth hole, Jones hit what golf writer Martin Davis termed "the most bizarre shot of the tournament

and the luckiest of [Jones's] career." Distracted by two spectators, Jones topped his ball, which skipped across the surface of the pond. The "lily pad shot" ended up a short pitch away from the green and Jones birdied the hole with a 4. Jones won the tournament in the fourth round with a score of 287 after sinking a forty-foot putt on the final hole. He had to wait an hour to learn that he had defeated Macdonald Smith by 2 strokes. Upon his return home, Atlanta Mayor I. N. Ragsdale presented Jones with a gold key to the city as a "symbol of affection of his friends and neighbors."

In late September, Jones traveled to Merion Cricket Club in Ardmore, Pennsylvania, for the U.S. Amateur, the last of the year's major tournaments. The crowds were so large that the U.S. Marine Corps had to guard Jones on the course. Jones defeated Eugene Homans on the eleventh hole in the finals, making Jones the first golfer to win all four major championships in a single year. When he returned to Atlanta, the city hosted a ticker-tape parade for their conquering hero. The journalists searched for words to adequately describe the accomplishment. *New York Times* writer William D. Richardson declared it "the

This miniature replica of the British Amateur trophy, presented to Bobby Jones by the members of the Royal and Ancient Golf Club of St. Andrews, is inscribed "Matchless in Skill and Chivalrous in Spirit." Old Tom Morris is perched on the top of the trophy. *1995.14.M3, Atlanta History Center; William F. Hull, photographer*

most triumphant journey that any man ever traveled in sport." George Trevor of the *New York Sun* called the feat the "Impregnable Quadrilateral of Golf," while O. B. Keeler of the *Atlanta Journal* termed it the "Grand Slam."

Jones's reflection on his fourth and final win revealed the strain of competition and foreshadowed his retirement:

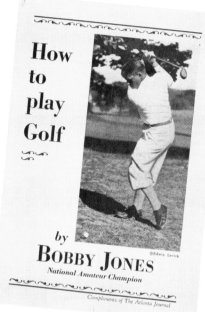

Jones authored *How to Play Golf* in 1924 after winning the U.S. Amateur. *Golf subject file, Atlanta History Center*

I felt the wonderful feeling of release from tension and relaxation that I had wanted so badly for so long a time. I wasn't quite certain what had happened or what I had done. I only knew that I had completed a period of most strenuous effort and that at this point, nothing more remained to be done, and that once I had completed this particular project, at least, there could never at any time in the future be anything else to do.

A little more than a month later, on November 17, 1930, at age twenty-eight, Jones surprised his fans and competitors by announcing his retirement from tournament golf to turn his attention to his family and law practice:

Fourteen years of intense tournament play in this country and abroad have given me all I wanted in the way of hard work in the game. I have reached the point where I felt that my profession required more of

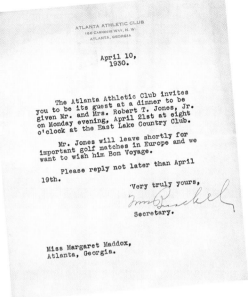

This letter invites Margaret Maddox to a dinner in honor of Mr. Jones's "important golf matches in Europe," which would become the first two legs of his Grand Slam. *Margaret Maddox Papers (MSS-952), Atlanta History Center*

my time and effort, leaving golf in its proper place, as a means of obtaining recreation and enjoyment.

Despite his public retirement, Jones continued to popularize the game for the next four decades. He wrote three books, became a regular contributor to Grantland Rice's *The American Golfer*, did a weekly half-hour radio show, and designed the first set of matched golf clubs for A. G. Spalding & Bros.

Jones's most public post-retirement contributions to the game were twelve one-reel films devoted to golf instruction. On November 13, 1930, the world's most famous golfer signed a contract with Warner Brothers to make *How I Play Golf*, a series of films that was "purely educational in character." The films were shown in theaters around the nation and featured well-known celebrities, including W. C. Fields, Warner Oland, James Cagney, and Edward G. Robinson. Sportswriter and friend O. B. Keeler helped write the scripts for the series—often on the set during the filming—and narrated several of the stories.

Jones is probably best remembered for establishing Augusta National Golf Club and the Masters tournament with Clifford Roberts, but he did not simply settle into the world of country club golf. On June 9, 1942, Jones was commissioned as a captain in the Army Air Force and served as an intelligence officer under General Dwight D. Eisenhower. A medical disability and his age (forty) did not compel him to go to war, but he insisted on serving.

This cigar was a gift for patrons at a New York City dinner on July 2, 1930, honoring Jones's British Open win.
Robert Tyre Jones Jr. Collection (1995.13.M4), Atlanta History Center; William F. Hull, photographer

He was honorably discharged as a Lieutenant Colonel in 1944.

In 1948, Jones was diagnosed with the degenerative spinal disease syringomyelia, leaving him unable to play the sport he so loved. Yet he remained active in the game. That same year, he helped found Peachtree Golf Club in Atlanta, one of the world's most renowned courses. In 1958, he returned to St. Andrews as the nonplaying team captain for the first World Amateur Team Championship. Jones had also been invited to accept the Freeman of the Royal Burgh of St. Andrews—the first American to receive this honor since Benjamin Franklin nearly two centuries earlier. Jones was presented with a silver casket and scroll that was adorned with the seal of the city. Upon receipt, Jones declared that "[t]his is the finest thing that's ever happened to me."

On December 18, 1971, at age sixty-nine, Bobby Jones died peacefully in his sleep. When they heard the news, golfers at St. Andrews stopped their play. The clubhouse flag was lowered to half-mast to honor one of the game's greatest ambassadors. Robert Tyre "Bobby" Jones Jr. was buried at a small, private ceremony in Oakland Cemetery in Atlanta on December 20, 1971. Today, almost three decades after his death, visitors still leave golf balls and tees at the gravesite, in a continuing tribute to the legendary golfer. ■

Born in 1902 on St. Patrick's Day, Jones was a frail child. *Special Collections Department, Robert W. Woodruff Library, Emory University*

Jones is pictured here (next to last row, third from left) at age thirteen
with his classmates from the Calhoun School on Atlanta's Piedmont Avenue.
Kenneth Thomas Photograph Collection (VIS-70f), Atlanta History Center

Jones played in his first national tournament,
the 1916 U.S. Amateur, at age fourteen.
Special Collections Department, Robert W. Woodruff Library, Emory University

Bobby Jones (far right) and Frank Godchaux (to Jones's right) at the 1922 Southern Amateur Championship at East Lake. Jones, who played the entire tournament with his left leg bandaged from a recent varicose vein operation, won. *Special Collections Department, Robert W. Woodruff Library, Emory University*

A match that will live long in the memory of the South—the victory of Bobby Jones and Perry Adair over Chick Evans and Ned Sawyer in 1917. *Hertzka-Mathewson Photograph Collection (HER-4-9A), Atlanta History Center*

Jimmy Maiden, Bobby Jones, Luke Ross (Jones's caddie), and Stewart Maiden at the
1923 U.S. Open at Inwood Country Club—where Jones won his first national title.
Special Collections Department, Robert W. Woodruff Library, Emory University

Jones returning home to Atlanta after his 1923 U.S. Open victory.
Special Collections Department, Robert W. Woodruff Library, Emory University

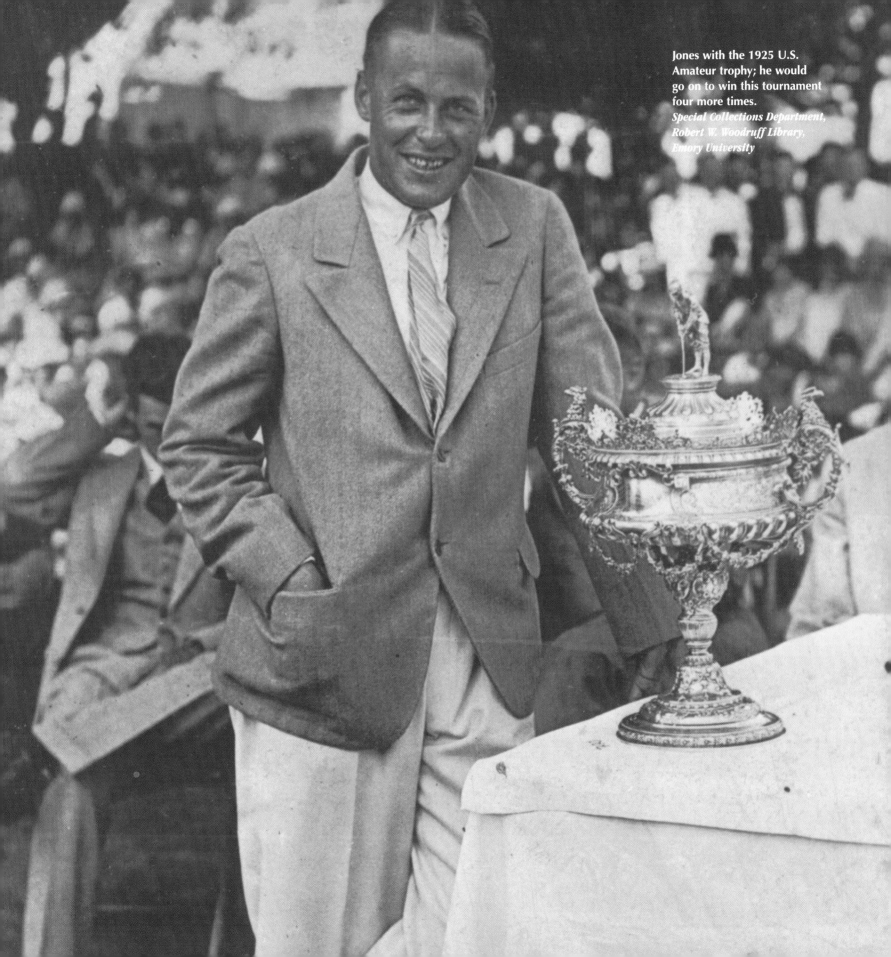

In 1926, Atlanta held a parade to honor Bobby Jones for winning the "double"—the U.S. Open and the British Open. *Kenneth G. Rogers Photographs (KGR-325-G), Atlanta History Center*

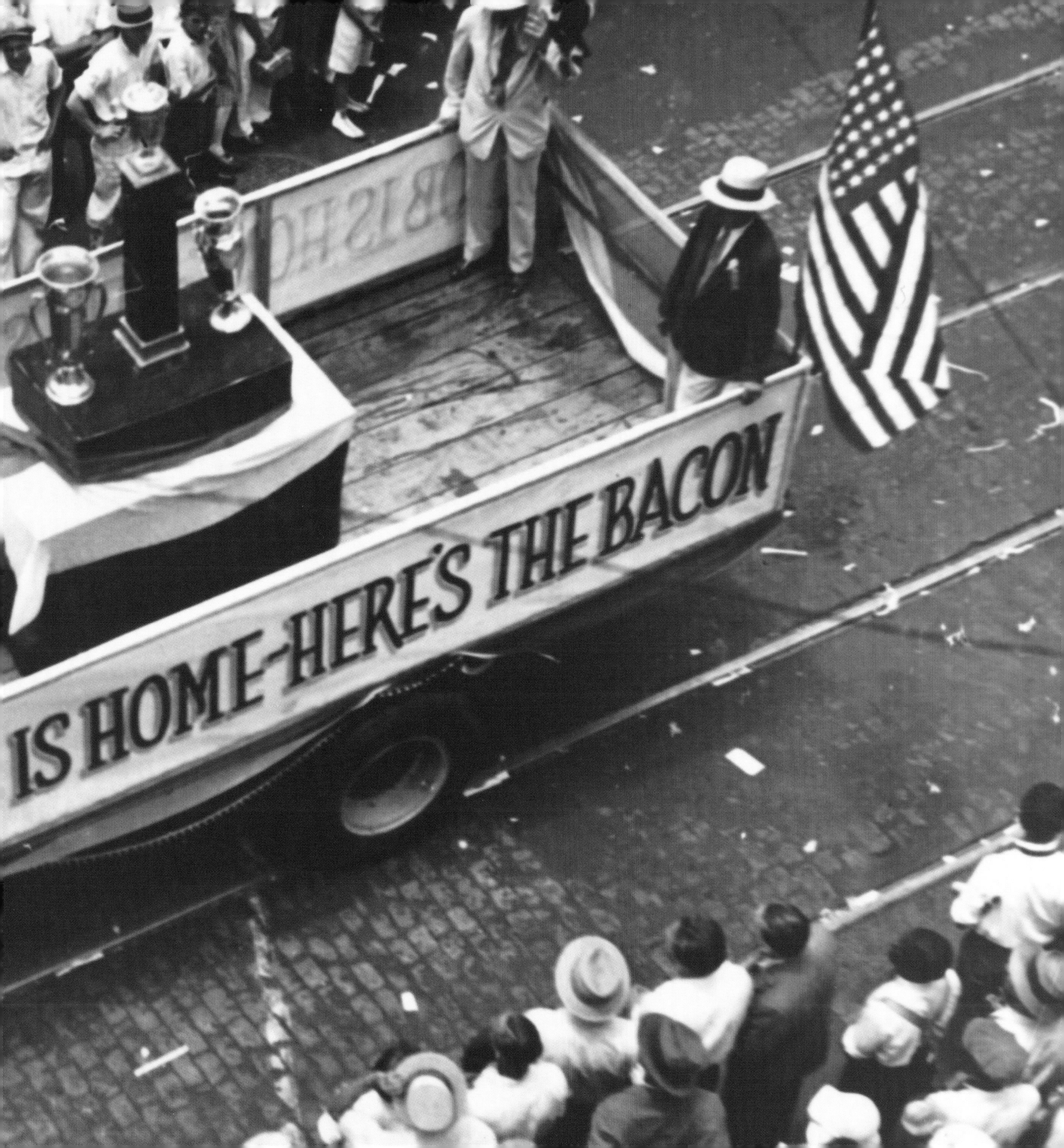
IS HOME–HERE'S THE BACON

Jones sunk his third birdie in a row on the fifth
hole of the 1927 National Amateur at Minikhada.
He broke the course record with a 142.
Special Collections Department, Robert W. Woodruff
Library, Emory University

Jones played and won the first leg of the
Grand Slam—the British Amateur—on the Old
Course at St. Andrews, his favorite course.
VIS-73, Atlanta History Center

**Jones putting on the tenth green during the first round of the
British Open Championship at Hoylake, June 18, 1930.**
Special Collections Department, Robert W. Woodruff Library, Emory University

Colonel, Mary, and Bob Jones returning from England, July 1930.
Jones Family

Jones returning to Atlanta after winning the Walker Cup, the British Amateur, and the British Open, 1930.
Special Collections Department, Robert W. Woodruff Library, Emory University

Grantland Rice declared that the 1930 U.S. Open was the "the greatest field ever assembled on any golf course."
Jones Family

Atlanta Journal-Constitution

Left to right: Mary and Bob Jones with Lawry Arnold. The Atlanta Athletic Club's East Lake facility held a dinner in Jones's honor after he won the Grand Slam. *Atlanta History Center, 1990.086*

On July 14, 1930, Atlanta hosted a ticker-tape parade for Jones after he won three of the four legs of the Grand Slam. *Kenneth G. Rogers Photograph Collection (ROG-6-29), Atlanta History Center*

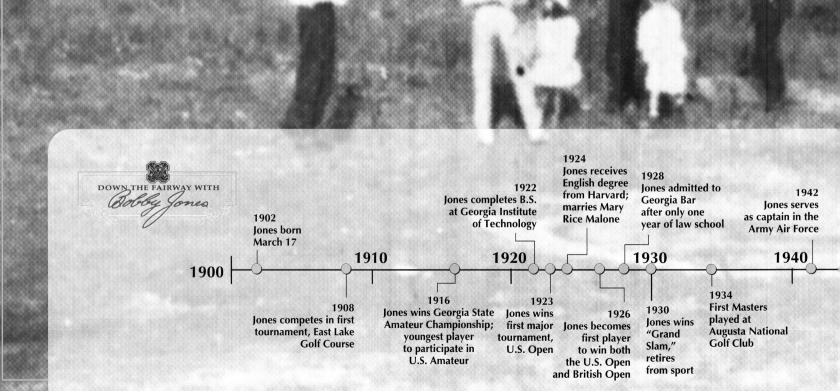

This is one of the earliest known photographs of the East Lake Golf Course. It was published in the *Golf and Tennis Record and Diary* in 1906 for Atlanta Athletic Club members.
Golf subject file, Atlanta History Center

DOWN THE FAIRWAY WITH
Bobby Jones

1900

1910

1920

1930

1940

1902
Jones born
March 17

1908
Jones competes in first
tournament, East Lake
Golf Course

1916
Jones wins Georgia State
Amateur Championship;
youngest player
to participate in
U.S. Amateur

1922
Jones completes B.S.
at Georgia Institute
of Technology

1923
Jones wins
first major
tournament,
U.S. Open

1924
Jones receives
English degree
from Harvard;
marries Mary
Rice Malone

1926
Jones becomes
first player
to win both
the U.S. Open
and British Open

1928
Jones admitted to
Georgia Bar
after only one
year of law school

1930
Jones wins
"Grand
Slam,"
retires
from sport

1934
First Masters
played at
Augusta National
Golf Club

1942
Jones serves
as captain in the
Army Air Force

CHAPTER 2

THE AGE OF THE AMATEUR

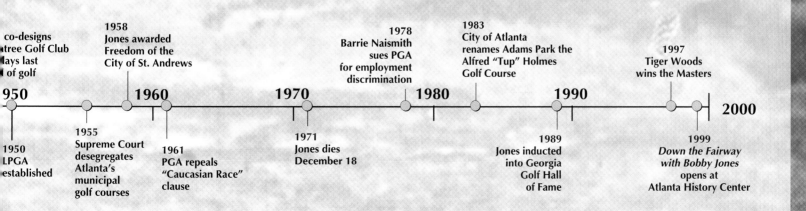

co-designs
tree Golf Club
lays last
of golf

1958
Jones awarded
Freedom of the
City of St. Andrews

1978
Barrie Naismith
sues PGA
for employment
discrimination

1983
City of Atlanta
renames Adams Park the
Alfred "Tup" Holmes
Golf Course

1997
Tiger Woods
wins the Masters

950   1960   1970   1980   1990   2000

1950
LPGA
established

1955
Supreme Court
desegregates
Atlanta's
municipal
golf courses

1961
PGA repeals
"Caucasian Race"
clause

1971
Jones dies
December 18

1989
Jones inducted
into Georgia
Golf Hall
of Fame

1999
*Down the Fairway
with Bobby Jones*
opens at
Atlanta History Center

"The essence of the man might well have been that he embodied the spirit of golf more than anyone who ever played the game." **JACK NICKLAUS**

The 1920s, referred to as the "Golden Age of American Sports," were dominated by legendary heroes—Babe Ruth in baseball, Jack Dempsey in boxing, Red Grange in football, Bill Tilden in tennis, and Robert Tyre "Bobby" Jones Jr. in golf. It was a time aptly described by sports reporters Allison Danzig and Peter Brandwein, who wrote in 1948: "Never before, or since, have so many transcendent performers arisen contemporaneously in almost every field of competitive athletics."

Thanks in part to the fame and success of Bobby Jones, golf enjoyed tremendous popularity and growth during this decade. In 1920, the United States Golf Association counted 477 member clubs; by the 1930s, there were more than 5,700 (about 4,500 of which were private). While a handful of players at these clubs competed for prize money, most felt as did Bobby Jones—that golf should be a leisure activity, a character-building sport played with friends and not for money. In *American Sports: From The Age of Folk Games to The Age of Televised Sports*, Benjamin Rader traces the history of this ideology. He argues that amateurism was inherited from upper-class English sportsmen and became the "cardinal principle of the American elite's sporting ideology." Amateur athletes embraced the tenets of "fair play" and were cautious not to seize advantages that were unavailable to their fellow competitors. "In principle, amateurs needed no game officials to enforce the rules; they policed themselves." Golf, then, was the quintessential amateur sport because adherence to the rules was the primary responsibility of the players. None symbolized this ideal better than Bobby Jones. In the foreword to Jones's autobiography *Down the Fairway*, published in 1927, Grantland Rice made this tribute to the young athlete:

Bobby Jones has been something more than one of the most skilled shot makers in the span of golf. Back of this amazing skill there have also been character, magnetism, courage, and intelligence of a high order. He has been the ideal sportsman in every contest, always scrupulous in observing not only the letter of the rules but the spirit of the game.

He inspired a generation to embrace amateur athletics and, as a result, the Age of the Amateur was, in many ways, the Age of Bobby Jones.

As with country clubs, amateur associations helped popularize golf in the early part of the century. These associations were based on sporting communities that helped promote track and field, boxing, swimming, wrestling, and tennis in the nineteenth century. In the 1880s, wealthy urbanites sought to divorce certain sports from their working-class, ethnic roots by establishing elite umbrella organizations such as the National Association of Amateur Athletes of America in 1879 and the Amateur Athletic Union in 1888. Individual sports also established their own governing bodies, including the United States Lawn Tennis Association (1881) and the United States Golf Association (1894). These national organizations were best represented by regional and state offices. The Georgia State Golf Association (GSGA), for example, was founded in 1914 to promote the integrity and traditions of the game of golf. Fourteen-year-old Bobby Jones won the GSGA's first Georgia Amateur Championship in 1916. Women's amateur associations served a similar purpose. Many of the best female golfers in Jones's home state of Georgia were members of the Atlanta Women's Golf Association (AWGA) and/or the Georgia Women's Golf Association (GWGA). The AWGA was founded in 1922 for "the purpose of promoting interest in golf and inter-club competition among the women of the association's member clubs," which initially included Ansley Golf Club, Atlanta Athletic Club (East Lake), Capital City Club, and the Druid Hills Golf Club. The statewide GWGA was founded by Eleanor Keeler, wife of sportswriter O. B. Keeler, in 1929, to "conduct an annual championship and maintain the best interests of the game of golf among female amateurs." Tournaments hosted by the GSGA, AWGA, and GWGA attracted some of the state's and the nation's most talented golfers.

Druid Hills Golf Club House

Atlanta

The Home of ALEXA STIRLING, "Little BOB" JONES and PERRY ADAIR

Welcomes You

ATLANTA is the ideal golfing city of America because of its six great courses, and incomparable climate that permits year-round golf, and its noteworthy hotel facilities.

Atlanta is "Golf Headquarters" these days and we'd like to have you here.— Any information will be gladly furnished on request.

ATLANTA CONVENTION BUREAU
ATLANTA GEORGIA

Atlanta golfer Alexa Stirling received top billing on this Atlanta Convention Bureau map. Bobby Jones's fame would soon eclipse Stirling's.
Golf subject file, Atlanta History Center

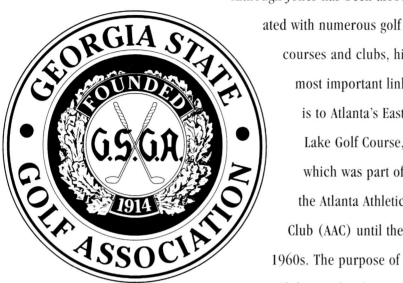

The Georgia State Golf Association was founded in 1914 to promote amateur golf.
Georgia State Golf Association

Although Jones has been associated with numerous golf courses and clubs, his most important link is to Atlanta's East Lake Golf Course, which was part of the Atlanta Athletic Club (AAC) until the 1960s. The purpose of the Club was clearly stated in its 1898 charter: "The object of this corporation is not pecuniary gain, but the formation of a social club, the special purpose of which is preparing and maintaining a gymnasium and enjoying physical exercise." Tennis, basketball, and swimming were the club's primary focus; golf did not become popular until 1905. John Heisman, later the Georgia Tech football coach for whom the Heisman Trophy was named, directed the club's athletic programs in 1908. George Adair, president of the AAC from 1905 to 1911, helped to popularize golf, overseeing the 1905 construction of the first golf course on a 187-acre plot in suburban DeKalb County's East Lake neighborhood. The site, owned by Athletic Club member Harry M. Atkinson, was originally an amusement park. Designed by Tom Bendelow, the first course had

just seven holes; it was expanded to eighteen in 1908. This original eighteen-hole golf course, the one on which Bobby Jones learned to play, was only in use until 1913, when golf course architect Donald Ross was hired to redesign it. Ross also designed an additional club course (known fondly to the club's members as "Number 2") in 1928. After two clubhouses were destroyed by fire, a third and final clubhouse was built by noted Atlanta architect Philip Trammell Shutze in 1926.

Bobby Jones played his first round of golf at East Lake at the age of six. After sneaking onto the course to watch club professional Stewart Maiden play, Jones would go home and mimic his swing. The practice paid off; Jones went on to win thirteen national championships in the United States and Great Britain, including the Grand Slam in 1930. Thanks to Jones's accomplishments, East Lake has become known throughout the golfing world.

While certainly the most famous, Bobby Jones was not East Lake's only outstanding golfer; the course has trained twenty-one regional and twenty-one national golf champions. The club's Alexa Stirling won the Women's National Amateur Championship in 1916, 1919, and 1920. Although few sports prior to the Civil War were deemed appropriate for women, golf, with its limited physical activity, was perceived as being "suited" to their genteel nature.

Magazines, such as *Frank Leslie's Popular Monthly* and the *Ladies Home Journal*, urged women to organize foursomes and play golf. The United States Golf Association's first Women's Amateur Championship was held in 1895 at Meadow Brook Club in Long Island and was won by Mrs. C. S. Brown. What Brown had in common with Alexa Stirling and her contemporaries who played golf prior to World War II was their backgrounds—wealthy and well-educated. Golf at this time was played mostly at country clubs with exclusive membership rosters. In 1898, H. L. Fitz Patrick, writing for *Outing* magazine, declared that golf "is a sport restricted to the richer classes of the country." Bobby Jones and his peers at East Lake, including Stirling, whose father was a Scottish physician who served as the British consul, easily fit into this category.

Stirling was also the first and only female golfer to ever beat Jones in competition. When she was twelve and he was six, the two golfers played in a six-hole neighborhood competition. Although Stirling recorded the lowest score, it was Jones who was awarded the trophy. Years later, Jones recalled, "I'll always believe Alexa won that cup . . ." Despite the error, Stirling became Atlanta's first golfer of national stature; an early Atlanta Convention Bureau map welcomes visitors to the "Home of Alexa Stirling, 'Little Bob' Jones, and Perry Adair" (another local amateur golfer known as the "Kid Wonder of Dixie"). In 1917,

Stirling, Jones, Adair, and Elaine Rosenthal of Chicago barnstormed the United States and played in exhibition matches for the Red Cross, raising $150,000 for the war effort. Seven years later, Stirling married, moved to Canada, and retired from tournament golf. She and Jones, though, sustained a lifelong friendship. Although

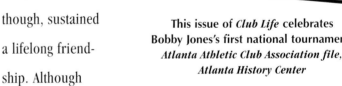

This issue of *Club Life* celebrates Bobby Jones's first national tournament. *Atlanta Athletic Club Association file, Atlanta History Center*

Jones later became the more famous golfer, it was Stirling and her contemporaries who blazed a trail for women golfers and began a rich legacy that has spanned more than a century.

Another of Jones's contemporaries, Watts Gunn, won several championships, including the Georgia Amateur (1923 and 1927), Southern Amateur (1928), and Southern Open (1928). He was the runner-up to Bobby Jones in the 1925

U.S. Amateur, the only instance in which two golfers from the same club have met in the finals of a national championship. The next year, Jones and Gunn competed against Andrew Jamieson and Cyril Tolley in the foursomes play in the Walker Cup, helping the U.S. win 6 to 5.

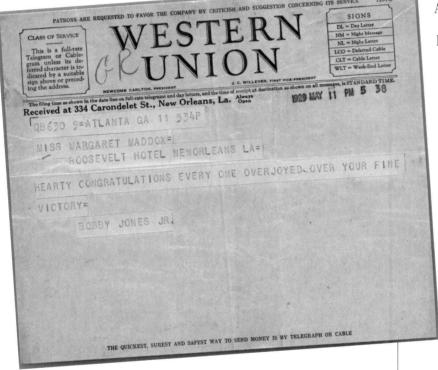

Jones sent this telegram to Margaret Maddox upon her victory in the 1929 Southern Women's Amateur.
Margaret Maddox Papers (MSS-952), Atlanta History Center

Jones's protégé, Charlie Yates, moved to East Lake with his family when he was four and perfected his game by watching Jones—just as Jones had done years earlier with Maiden. Also like Jones, Yates had a distinguished amateur career, winning the Georgia Amateur in 1931,

the Western Amateur in 1935, and the British Amateur in 1938. Yates played in eleven Masters Tournaments, on two Walker Cup teams, and in nine U.S. Amateur championships. He has been the secretary of Augusta National Golf Club since the 1950s, and in 1980 he was awarded the most prestigious honor in golf—the Bob Jones Award. Yates proudly refers to the award as his most prized accomplishment.

East Lake's other notable golfers include Dorothy Kirby, winner of the Georgia Women's Championship in 1933 (at age thirteen, notable enough for mention in the *Guinness Book of World Records*), the Women's Southern in 1937, the Titleholders Championship in 1941 and 1942, and the North and South Women's Amateur Championship in 1943. Jones coached Kirby prior to her victory at the U.S. Women's Amateur in 1951. Although Margaret Maddox never won a national title, she, too, had a distinguished amateur career, winning the Southern Women's Amateur Championship in 1929 and the Georgia Women's Amateur in 1931, 1932, and 1938. She qualified and played in the U.S. Women's Amateur four times (1933, 1934, 1939, and 1950). Similar to Yates and Kirby, Maddox benefited from the mentoring of Bobby Jones.

East Lake's Tommy Barnes qualified for the U.S. Amateur sixteen straight times, won the Bobby Jones Four Ball Meet and the Dogwood Tournament five times each, and won the Georgia Amateur in 1941.

East Lake also was home to some of the most accomplished teaching professionals in the state, including Stewart Maiden (Bobby Jones's mentor) and George, Harold, and Jack Sargent. George Sargent (1882–1962) was born in Dorking, England, won the 1909 U.S. Open, and was a member of the PGA at its inception in 1916 (he served as president from 1921 to 1926). In 1932, Bobby Jones brought him to East Lake where he served as the club professional until 1947. An accomplished club-maker, George also introduced the use of motion pictures in the study of the golf swing, using Jones as his model. Harold Sargent (1913–1990) succeeded his father as head professional at East Lake in 1947 (a position he held until 1978) and also served as PGA president (from 1958 to 1960); George and Harold are the only father-son combination to have held this post in the association's history. Harold is best remembered for bringing the Ryder Cup Matches to East Lake in 1963. In 1979, his brother Jack (1924–1985) became the professional at East Lake and served until 1985. Jack was a member of the PGA for twenty-six years and was actively involved in junior golf. He was a premier expert on the

rules of golf, officiating The Players Championship for eleven years and the Ryder Cup for three.

Because of poor health, Bobby Jones played his last round of golf at East Lake—with Tommy Barnes, Bob Ingram, and Henry Lindner—in 1948. Jones, however, remained an active member of the Atlanta Athletic Club. Beginning in the early 1950s, a steadily increasing number of the membership clamored for the club to relocate, a reflection of the membership's population shift toward Atlanta's northern suburbs and a growing concern over crime in the East Lake neighborhood. In 1966, the AAC sold the "Number 2" course to raise funds for a new facility; the site then became East Lake Meadows, a public housing project. Soon after, the members turned their energies toward building anew in north Fulton County. A twenty-seven-hole course and new clubhouse opened in the Duluth community in 1967.

But not everyone was pleased with the Athletic Club's move to the suburbs. In 1968, twenty-five dissatisfied AAC members, intent on carrying on an East Lake golfing tradition, raised the money to buy their original course and clubhouse. There, they began the East Lake Country Club. In 1994, the club was purchased once again, this time by Atlanta real estate developer Tom Cousins, who renamed it the East Lake Golf Club. Cousins wished to recreate the classic club of the 1920s, redefine the area's public housing, and strengthen the East Lake community. Cousins donated the club to the nonprofit CF Foundation—but only on the condition that it be restored as a tribute to Bobby Jones and used as a catalyst to revitalize the surrounding neighborhood.

Towards Cousins's goal, noted golf architect Rees Jones restored the course to the original 1913 Donald Ross design. He then renovated the 1926 clubhouse and filled it with Bobby Jones artifacts and other golfing memorabilia. While the revamped course and clubhouse are still private, a new eighteen-hole public golf course (located on the site of the former "Number 2" course and East Lake Meadows), named after golfing great Charlie Yates, forms the centerpiece of the redeveloped community. The East Lake Junior Golf Academy, an after-school educational program, operates at the new Yates course, using golf to teach students principles of hard work, integrity, and self-discipline. And with a new mixed-income public housing development being built just next door, East Lake might once again nurture a neighborhood youth into the sport's next Grand Slam champion. ∎

BOB JONES AWARD WINNERS

In 1955, the United States Golf Association established the Bob Jones Award to honor a person who, by a single act or over the years, emulates Jones's sportsmanship, respect for the game and its rules, generosity of spirit, sense of fair play, and perhaps even sacrifice.

1955—Francis Ouimet
1956—William C. Campbell
1957—Mildred D. Zaharias
1958—Margaret Curtis
1959—Findlay S. Douglas
1960—Charles Evans Jr.
1961—Joseph B. Carr
1962—Horton Smith
1963—Patty Berg
1964—Charles R. Coe
1965—Glenna Collett Vare
1966—Gary Player
1967—Richard S. Tufts
1968—Robert R. Dickson
1969—Gerald H. Micklem
1970—Roberto De Vicenzo
1971—Arnold Palmer
1972—Michael Bonallack
1973—Gene Littler
1974—Byron Nelson
1975—Jack Nicklaus
1976—Ben Hogan
1977—Joseph C. Dey Jr.
1978—Bing Crosby & Bob Hope
1979—Tom Kite
1980—Charles R. Yates
1981—JoAnne Gunderson Carter
1982—William J. Patton
1983—Marueen Ruttle Garrett
1984—R. Jay Sigel
1985—Fuzzy Zoeller
1986—Jess W. Sweerser
1987—Tom Watson
1988—Isaac B. Grainger
1989—Chi Chi Rodriguez
1990—Peggy Kirk Bell
1991—Ben Crenshaw
1992—Gene Sarazen
1993—P. J. Boatwright Jr.
1994—Lewis Oehmig
1995—Herbert Warren Wind
1996—Betsy Rawls
1997—Fred Brand Jr.
1998—Nancy Lopez
1999—Ed Updegraff

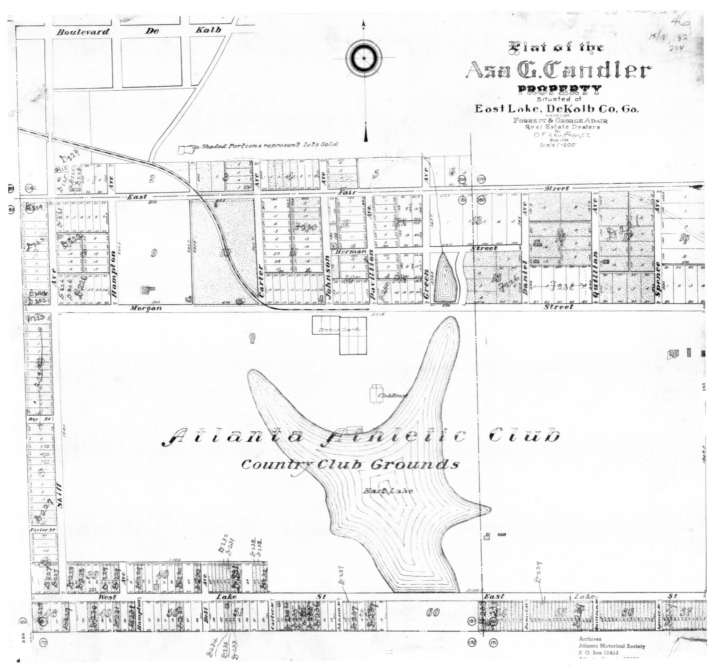

In 1906, Asa G. Candler, the founder of The Coca-Cola Company, sold land lots to perspective homeowners who wanted to live near the Atlanta Athletic Club's new golf course.
Plat Maps, District 15, Land Lot 181, Atlanta History Center

Athletic Club House, East Lake, Atlanta, Ga.

This East Lake clubhouse was built to replace an earlier one that burned.
Unfortunately, this clubhouse, too, would burn in 1925.
Postcard Collection (PCC-228), Atlanta History Center

The third East Lake clubhouse was built in 1926.
Postcard Collection (PCC-231), Atlanta History Center

Jones with Stewart Maiden, Harrison Johnston, and Leo Diegel at the Inverness Golf Club, Toledo, Ohio. The Scottish Maiden earned the nickname "Kiltie the King Maker," due to the success of two of his pupils, Jones and Alexa Stirling. *United States Golf Association*

Alexa Stirling, Georgia's first golfer of national stature, blazed a trail for both men and women in the state. Alexa is shown fourth from the left.
Sandy Carwardine and the Atlanta Athletic Club

Atlanta's most famous golfers, Bobby Jones and Alexa Stirling, ca. 1923. *Kenneth G. Rogers Photograph Collection (COL-108-2), Atlanta History Center*

Atlanta Athletic Club member H. M. Atkinson (second from left), who owned the land
East Lake was built upon, and Bobby Jones, ca. 1920s.
J.P. Dick Collection (DIC-1-11A), Atlanta History Center

**Although known primarily as a sportswriter, O. B. Keeler was
also an accomplished amateur golfer.**
Keeler Family and Marietta Museum of History

"They talked about dogs, not golf or baseball." Ty Cobb, Herschel Cobb, and Bobby Jones, near Waynesboro, Georgia, in 1925. *Hertzka-Mathewson Photograph Collection (HER-3-11), Atlanta History Center*

**Bobby Jones defeated fellow Atlanta Athletic Club member Watts Gunn
in the finals of the 1925 U.S. Amateur.**
Sidney L. Matthew

e Yates with the 1938
Amateur trophy.
s R. Yates

Dorothy Kirby began her golfing career by winning the Georgia Women's Amateur at age thirteen, notable enough for inclusion in the *Guiness Book of World Records*.
Dorothy Kirby

Tommy Barnes, an accomplished amateur and friend of Bobby Jones.
Kenneth G. Rogers Photographs (KGR-180-15), Atlanta History Center

Atlanta golfer Charlie Yates, namesake of a new public eighteen-hole golf course adjacent to the East Lake Golf Club, with children from the East Lake Junior Golf Academy.
East Lake Community Foundation

Golf professional Leon Gilmore works with students of the East Lake Junior Golf Academy.
East Lake Community Foundation

East Lake Golf Club began a caddie
program to help teach young
players the rules of the game.
East Lake Community Foundation

The Charlie Yates Golf Course was dedicated on September 14, 1998.
Golf subject file (1999.46), Atlanta History Center

Tiger Woods hit the first shot at the opening of the Charlie Yates Golf Course. *Atlanta History Center; Catherine Lewis, photographer*

The current Augusta National clubhouse was a private residence built at the end of the Civil War.
Jones Family

DOWN THE FAIRWAY WITH
Bobby Jones

1902
Jones born
March 17

1908
Jones competes in first tournament, East Lake Golf Course

1916
Jones wins Georgia State Amateur Championship; youngest player to participate in U.S. Amateur

1922
Jones completes B.S. at Georgia Institute of Technology

1923
Jones wins first major tournament, U.S. Open

1924
Jones receives English degree from Harvard; marries Mary Rice Malone

1926
Jones becomes first player to win both the U.S. Open and British Open

1928
Jones admitted to Georgia Bar after only one year of law school

1930
Jones wins "Grand Slam," retires from sport

1934
First Masters played at Augusta National Golf Club

1942
Jones serves as captain in the Army Air Force

1900   **1910**   **1920**   **1930**   **1940**

CHAPTER 3

BOBBY JONES'S ARCHITECTURAL LEGACY

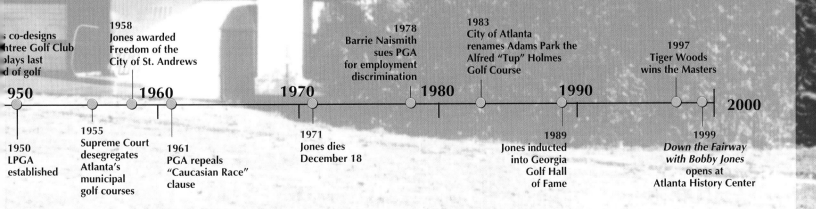

*"No man learns to design a golf course simply
by playing golf, no matter how well."* **BOBBY JONES**

After winning the Grand Slam in 1930 and retiring from tournament golf, Bobby Jones became interested in building an "ideal" golf course. Jones's entree into golf course design had begun just a few years earlier at North Carolina's Highlands Country Club, just about three hours northeast of his Atlanta home. There, in 1928, a group that included Jones, his father, Scott Hudson (the Atlanta Athletic Club's manager), and Sam Evins hired East Lake architect Donald Ross to build the new course. It soon became a popular mountain retreat.

Jones was anxious to further apply his philosophy of golf course architecture. So, with the support of Clifford Roberts, an investment banker from New York whom Jones had befriended in the 1920s, and upon the advice of Thomas Barrett Jr., an Augusta, Georgia, businessman, Jones decided to build his course in Augusta, in his home state of Georgia. The town boasted a milder climate than Atlanta, making it more conducive to winter golf, but more importantly, Jones had found there what he felt was the perfect piece of property. As he later wrote in *Golf Is My Game*, "It seemed that this land had been lying here for

years just waiting for someone to lay a golf course upon it."

The site for Augusta National Golf Club was a 365-acre plot with a rich horticultural history on the west side of town. In 1854, Dennis Redmond established an indigo plantation on the site. When the business failed a couple of years later, he sold the land to Belgian nobleman Louis Matheiu Edouard Berckmans. Baron Berckmans and his son, Prosper Jules Alphonse, formed P. J. Berckmans Company and began operating the Fruitlands Nursery. The nursery grew many varieties of exotic fruit trees, flowering shrubs, and flowers for distribution around the country. But Prosper Berckmans died in 1910, and Fruitlands floundered soon after. In 1925 the land was soon sold to a Miami developer who hoped to transform the nursery into a golf resort—until he went bankrupt. When Jones and Roberts inspected the property in 1930, it had not been in use for more than a decade.

In 1931, the property was purchased for seventy thousand dollars, and an organizational committee of five men, including Jones, was assembled to build the golf club. Jones selected Dr. Alister MacKenzie, an architect who shared Jones's vision of golf course design, as the course's builder. An English physician with a Scottish lineage, MacKenzie began his career as a golf course architect in 1907 and went on to design some of the world's most famous courses, including Cypress Point in California and the West Course at the Royal Melbourne Golf Course in Australia. MacKenzie's courses were patterned after the great Scottish and English courses, which meant they utilized natural advantages and minimized artificiality. Jones and MacKenzie aimed to create a course that would challenge the best players while providing maximum enjoyment to the rest. In *Golf Is My Game*, Jones explained, "We hope to make bogeys easy, if frankly sought, pars readily obtainable by standard good play, and birdies, except on par-five holes, dearly bought." To this end, they created wide fairways with few bunkers and large greens. The result, according to architect Robert Trent Jones, was " . . . a thinking man's course." The course was completed in December 1932 and opened the next month. Unfortunately, MacKenzie died in 1934 and never saw the tournament that would make his creation famous.

The golf course has undergone many alterations since it first opened, starting in 1934 when Bobby Jones reversed the front and back nines; the "new" order is still played

today. Several noted architects have helped update and renovate the course, including Perry Maxwell; George Cobb, a native of Georgia who improved the main course and designed the par-3 course; Robert Trent Jones; George Fazio; Joe Finger; and Tom Fazio. Golfers Byron Nelson, Ben Hogan, and Jack Nicklaus have also been involved in improving specific holes. Augusta National's design has

Fruitlands Nurseries catalogs indicate the scope of the Berckmans operation.
Berckmans Collection, Cherokee Garden Library, Atlanta History Center

inspired hundreds of copies, leading golf writer and historian Herbert Warren Wind to call it "the most influential golf course in America."

The Augusta National Golf Club is so named because its members come from throughout the United States and from several foreign countries. During the Club's first years, members were individuals who were acquainted with a member of the organizing committee, most notably

Jones. The first members, an affluent and diverse group that included Robert Woodruff (the chairman of The Coca-Cola Company), sportswriter Grantland Rice, and Alfred Severin Bourne (the heir to the Singer Sewing Machine empire), used Augusta as an exclusive retreat. Among the most famous of the later members was Dwight D. Eisenhower, who first visited Augusta National in 1948 while still General of the Army. He befriended Clifford Roberts and Bobby Jones during that first visit, and after he became a member of the club and President of the United States, Augusta came to be his favorite vacation destination.

But despite these big names, the club's founders had problems recruiting members, especially during the Depression. In *The Making of the Masters*, David Owen details how, in September 1931, Jones wrote dozens of letters to close friends to solicit support:

I am particularly anxious to interest my own friends in this project to get them to come down and play the course and take an interest in the club. I am therefore writing you to ask if you will not join this club and serve on its board of governors. I know you can be of assistance to us in getting the kind of members we want.

Despite Jones's plea and a vigorous membership drive, the club had only secured sixty-six memberships by April 1932; over the next two years, only ten additional members joined. (There are currently about three hundred members.) The golf club associated with the game's most famous competitor, indeed, had a slow start. A single tournament, though, would change everything.

The Augusta National Invitation Tournament, now known as "the Masters," was first played on March 22, 1934. What started as a friendly game between gentlemen has become a major cultural and sporting event that surpasses anything its founders could have imagined. Indeed, the Masters only came about after Roberts's bid for Augusta National to host the 1934 U.S. Open was rejected; he then decided to start his own tournament to help attract members and raise much-needed funds. When the name "Masters" was first proposed, Bobby

Jones thought it too pretentious and vetoed the idea; in 1938, he finally relented and the name was permanently, and officially, adopted. Tickets for the first tournament cost two dollars, and thirty-five hundred spectators came out to see Bobby Jones play golf, eight years after his retirement. Ralph Stonehouse, a professional player from Indiana, struck the first shot of the Masters. On the first day of the tournament, the *Atlanta Journal* reported, "Jones Off in His Putting As Masters Starts." Jones finished in thirteenth place, shooting 76-74-72-72-294. In his twelve appearances in the tournament he never broke par. Horton Smith, the first Masters champion, was awarded five thousand dollars (compiled from the donations of seventeen club members)—a modest purse even in 1934. Only the first twelve finishers were paid. In 1940, at Grantland Rice's suggestion, the board rescheduled the tournament for early April to accommodate sportswriters returning from baseball spring training in Florida—a tradition that continues today. The onset of World War II, however, interrupted the Masters, and Augusta National was forced to close. To contribute to the war effort, the club was transformed into a pasture for cattle and turkeys. Then, with the help of forty-two German prisoners of war housed at nearby Fort Gordon, Augusta National was restored and reopened in April 1946.

The first Masters was primarily a social affair (as it often is today among spectators). Jones invited players " . . . because of their past accomplishments in the game, their present stature, their promise, or even upon my own feeling of friendship for them." But this system soon proved too difficult to manage, and by 1935 the Club's board was forced to establish qualification guidelines, issuing invitations to:

Present and past U.S. Open champions

Present and past U.S. Amateur champions

Present and past British Amateur champions

Present and past British Open champions

Present and past U.S. PGA champions

Present members of the Ryder Cup team

Present members of the Walker Cup team

Over the past six decades the qualifications have changed and, despite Jones's legacy in amateur golf, amateur participation has declined dramatically; tournament golf since World War II has been dominated by professionals, and the Masters is no exception. In 1999, only six amateur players were invited to compete in the tournament (they included Matt Kuchar, who, like Bobby Jones before him, was an amateur from Atlanta and a student at Georgia Tech).

Although Jones respected all of his competitors, he also believed that the growing professionalism of golf threatened the survival of the sport. In a 1968 letter to Atlanta golfer Charlie Harrison, Jones espoused his philosophy:

There seems to be little appreciation today that golf is an amateur game, developed and supported by those who love to play it. Amateurs have built great golf courses where the playing pros play for so much money; amateurs maintain the clubs and public links organizations that provide jobs for working pros; amateurs spend millions of dollars each year on golf equipment and clothing and amateurs rule and administer the game on both sides of the Atlantic. In this way, golf has prospered for centuries. It would appear to be the best possible arrangement.

Augusta National jacket.
Charles R. Yates/
Atlanta History Center; William F. Hull,
photographer

Professionals were not the only golfers to bear the brunt of prejudice. African Americans had a hard time breaking into the game, for many private golf clubs and tournaments, including Augusta National and the Masters, were reluctant to desegregate. It was not until 1975, fourteen years after the PGA dropped their "Caucasian Race" clause that excluded African Americans from joining the organization, that Lee Elder broke the color barrier at the Masters. In the past several years, the club has accepted two African American members. Although one of the most visible symbols of prejudice in sports, Augusta National's story is not that unusual; for years, golf was a game that actively practiced segregation. While there were significant challenges to the sport's status quo, it was not until after a decade of intense scrutiny, ending with Tiger Woods's Masters victory in 1997, that golf began to fundamentally challenge its legacy of exclusion. In recent years, golf organizations, associations, and tournaments have sought to democratize the game.

PEACHTREE GOLF CLUB

Interested in building a club closer to his Atlanta home, Bobby Jones, with the help of Dick Garlington (a member of the USGA Greens Section and the Atlanta Athletic Club's Greens Committee) and several of their colleagues, founded the Atlanta Golf Club (now the Peachtree Golf Club) in the Brookhaven neighborhood of northeast Atlanta. Robert Trent Jones was selected as architect for the course, which opened in 1948. Similar to Augusta National, the club was inspired by Scottish and English golf links and was designed to "test the expert player and yet be enjoyable for the less capable player."

Bobby Jones and his colleagues had held the club's first organizational meeting on September 5, 1946. Plans were drawn to buy out the DeKalb Heights Corporation, which had begun construction on a golf club on 240 acres of land that was once an antebellum plantation. Located on Atlanta's Land Lot 277, the land was originally bought at a public auction in 1852 by Samual House for six hundred dollars. House built a home (which serves as Peachtree's current clubhouse) in 1857 from local trees and slave-made bricks. On July 18, 1864, during the Civil War's Atlanta Campaign, the home was commandeered for General William T. Sherman's overnight headquarters. After the war, Samual House returned to the property and lived there until his death in 1873. The property subsequently passed through several owners before being bought by William T. Ashford, who, with his son-in-law H. Cobb Caldwell, established Ashford Park Nurseries on the site. Ashford died in 1931 and Caldwell operated the business until it was sold to the Atlanta Golf Club founders in 1945.

The Berckmans family operated Fruitlands Nurseries, future site of Augusta National Golf Club, for nearly half a century. *Berckmans Collection, Cherokee Garden Library, Atlanta History Center*

The organizers of the Atlanta Golf Club proposed an initial limit of 150 members, each of whom would subscribe two thousand dollars, plus taxes, for the capital stock of the new club corporation. Eighty "acceptable" members were invited to join the 70 stockholders of DeKalb Heights to comprise the charter membership of the new golf club, which was incorporated on March 8, 1947, with the support of 105 petitioners. The club's name was officially changed to Peachtree Golf Club the following year.

Bobby Jones and his colleagues selected Robert Trent Jones, then the leading golf course designer from New York, as architect for the course because "his conception of golf course architecture so perfectly agreed with our own." Trent Jones himself explained that in designing Peachtree, he was guided by the conception of golf course architecture pioneered at Augusta National. The 240 acres permitted him to create a course that had "ample room between fairways and ample opportunity to lengthen the holes should there be any great change in the driving power of the ball." The planning of the course began in May 1945, and construction began in February 1946. Bobby Jones helped plan every obstacle; during construction, he hit dozens of balls on the newly bulldozed fairways to test the position of the hazards. The first nine holes opened for play in October 1947; the second nine were ready in July 1948. The 7,043-yard course features large fairways, ample roughs, and dozens of trees to frame each hole. Although an intensely private club, Peachtree opened its doors to host the Walker Cup Matches in 1989. Peachtree Golf Club is often ranked as one of the nation's best golf courses by *Golf Magazine* and *Golf Digest*. Today, both the Augusta National and Peachtree Golf Clubs stand as living memorials to Jones's skills as a golf course designer. ■

Fruitlands Nurseries' influence is still felt at Augusta National. Alister MacKenzie preserved the foliage, recognizing the botanical significance of trees, shrubs, and flowering plants—some of which are not found anywhere else in the United States—on this now-famous site. The thousands of miles of Amur privet hedge that grow throughout the nation can be traced to the hedge behind Augusta National's practice tee. Out of respect for the land's horticultural heritage, the holes at Augusta are named for flowering trees:

1	Tea Olive	par 4
2	Pink Dogwood	par 5
3	Flowering Peach	par 4
4	Flowering Crab Apple	par 3
5	Magnolia	par 4
6	Juniper	par 3
7	Pampas	par 4
8	Yellow Jasmine	par 5
9	Carolina Cherry	par 4
10	Camellia	par 4
11	White Dogwood	par 4
12	Golden Bell	par 3
13	Azalea	par 5
14	Chinese Fir	par 4
15	Firethorn	par 5
16	Redbud	par 3
17	Nandina	par 4
18	Holly	par 4

At age seventy-four, Louis Berckmans, son of P. J. Berckmans, returned to Augusta to help rehabilitate the trees and shrubs and was made an honorary member of the club. Though never formally associated with the original nursery, his younger brother Allie also returned to become Augusta National's site manager.

Bobby Jones, ready for tennis at Highlands Country Club in North Carolina, ca. 1930s.
State Normal School Photograph Collection (VIS-74), Atlanta History Center

Part of the ornamental garden at Fruitlands Nursery, ca. 1917.
Berckmans Collection, Cherokee Garden Library, Atlanta History Center

Jones with golf course engineer Wendell P. Miller at Augusta National, 1931.
Atlanta History Center

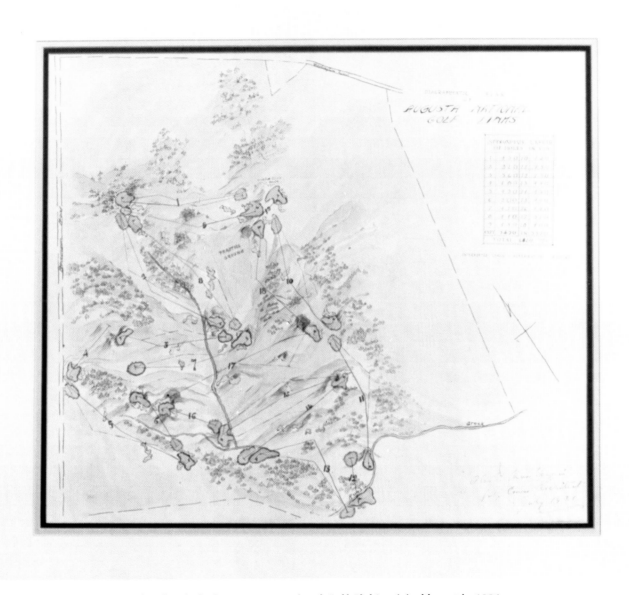

This sketch depicts Augusta National Golf Club's original layout in 1931.
Alston & Bird

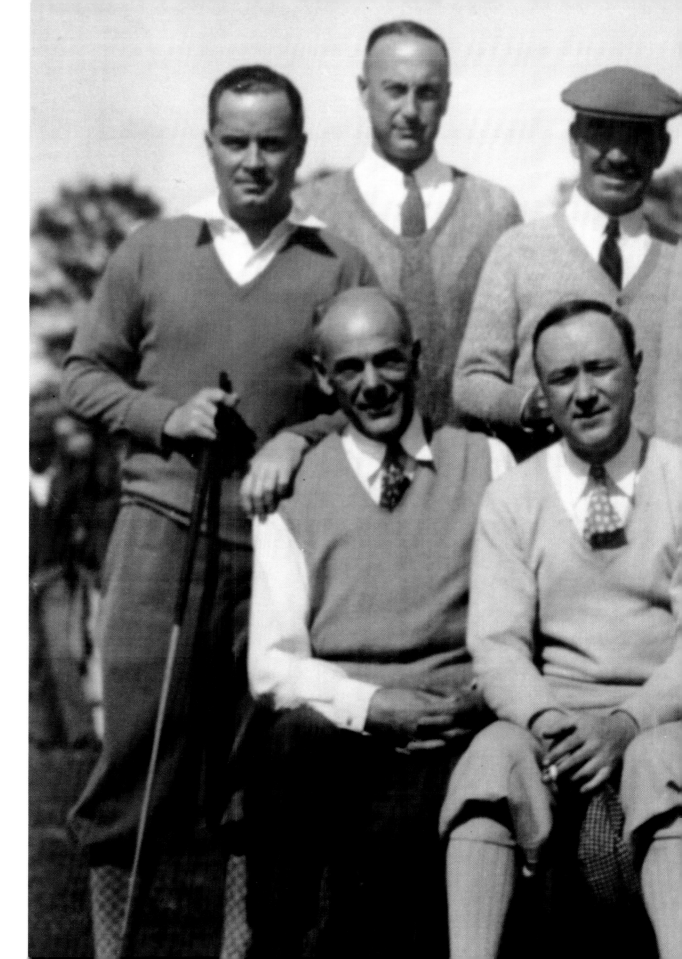

Augusta National attracted some of the most influential businessmen in the nation, including M. H. Aylesworth, the president of NBC (second from left, seated), and Alfred Severin Bourne, the Singer sewing machine magnate (fifth from left, standing). *Special Collections Department, Robert W. Woodruff Library, Emory University*

Jones with Horton Smith, the first Masters
Champion, 1934. Smith won again in 1936.
*Kenneth G. Rogers Photograph Collection
(COL-33-1), Atlanta History Center*

Jones in his Augusta National green jacket. The embroidered logo
on his pocket was only used for a few years.
Special Collections Department, Robert W. Woodruff Library,
Emory University

NUMBER 11　　　　　　　　　"WHITE DOGWOOD"　　　　　　　　　PAR 4 445 YARDS

NUMBER 12　　　　　　　　　"GOLDEN BELL"　　　　　　　　　PAR 3 155 YARDS

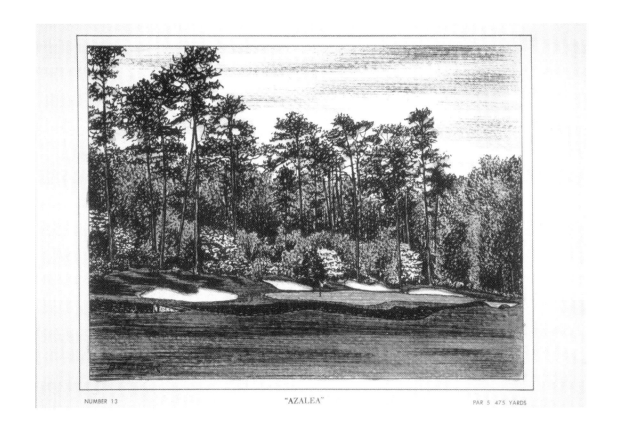

NUMBER 13   "AZALEA"   PAR 5 475 YARDS

**Mark Baltzegar's watercolor drawings of White Dogwood (11), The Golden Bell (12), and Azalea (13)
comprise Amen Corner, reportedly the most difficult holes on the Augusta National course.**
Special Collections Department, Robert W. Woodruff Library, Emory University

Bobby Jones with the Duke of Windsor at Augusta National Golf Club, May 18, 1952.
Kenneth G. Rogers Photographs (KGR-240-1), Atlanta History Center

Ben Hogan helping Sam Snead put on the green jacket in 1952. Clifford Roberts is on the left; Jones is in the foreground.
Kenneth G. Rogers Photographs (KGR-253-1), Atlanta History Center

Augusta National during the Masters, April 10, 1960.
Kenneth G. Rogers Photographs (KGR-260-6), Atlanta History Center

Caddies at Augusta National, March 30, 1952.
Kenneth G. Rogers Photographs (KGR-261-1), Atlanta History Center

Robert Snodgrass and Jones at the opening of a presidential campaign kick-off for Dwight D. Eisenhower.
Special Collections Department, Robert W. Woodruff Library, Emory University

President Dwight D. Eisenhower painted this likeness of Jones based on an original painting by Thomas A. Stephens. This limited-edition lithograph of Eisenhower's painting was signed by Eisenhower and Jones.
Robert Tyre Jones Jr. Visual Arts Collection (1995.014), Atlanta History Center

Charlie Yates (left) comparing the Thomas Stephens lithograph with President Eisenhower's reproduction. *Special Collections Department, Robert W. Woodruff Library, Emory University*

Jones with Peachtree
Golf Club architect
Robert Trent Jones
(on far right) and five of
the earliest members.
Peachtree Golf Club

Bobby Jones's birthday party,
March 1954, Peachtree Golf Club.
J. Hixson Kinsella Photographs
(1978.475), Atlanta History Center

Louise Suggs won nearly every tournament in women's golf and remains one of the sport's most accomplished athletes.
Mrs. O.B. Keeler Photographs (VIS-72), Atlanta History Center

DOWN THE FAIRWAY WITH
Bobby Jones

1902
Jones born
March 17

1908
Jones competes in first
tournament, East Lake
Golf Course

1910

1916
Jones wins Georgia State
Amateur Championship;
youngest player
to participate in
U.S. Amateur

1922
Jones completes B.S.
at Georgia Institute
of Technology

1920

1923
Jones wins
first major
tournament,
U.S. Open

1924
Jones receives
English degree
from Harvard;
marries Mary
Rice Malone

1926
Jones becomes
first player
to win both
the U.S. Open
and British Open

1928
Jones admitted to
Georgia Bar
after only one
year of law school

1930
Jones wins
"Grand
Slam,"
retires
from sport

1930

1934
First Masters
played at
Augusta National
Golf Club

1942
Jones serves
as captain in the
Army Air Force

1940

1900

CHAPTER 4

THE MAKING OF A MODERN GAME

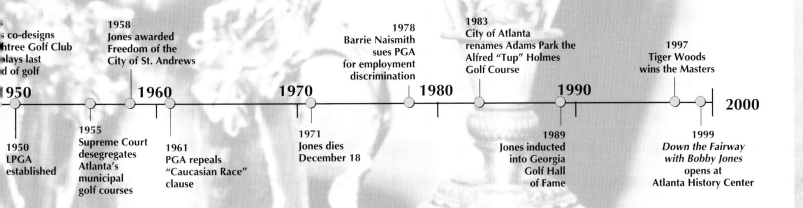

*"The game of golf may be an equalizer,
but it has never been egalitarian."* **ROBINSON HOLLOWAY**

Golf changed dramatically in the decades after Bobby Jones's 1930 retirement. While Jones himself did not provoke the transformation, he helped bridge the early and modern eras in American golf and deserves credit for popularizing golf among players of all races and social classes.

Originally, golf was a much more inclusive and democratic sport, popular

Two years after the Bobby Jones Golf Course opened, Margaret Maddox gathered a foursome of other accomplished female golfers, including Rosalie Mayer, a Jewish golfer.
Margaret Maddox Papers (MSS-952), Atlanta History Center

with men and women of different ranks. Members of the royal family played golf, but so did Scottish tradesmen and apprentices. It was only after it spread to England and the United States in the nineteenth century that golf became increasingly associated with the elite. Before World War II, the era dominated by Jones, golf was almost exclusively played on private courses that were largely restricted to wealthy, white members—African American, Jewish, and female golfers were denied full membership to most of these clubs.

In response to such exclusion, these groups developed their own clubs. Jewish players in Atlanta, for example, had the Standard Club, which had been originally founded in 1867 as the Concordia Association by a group of German Jews. In 1946 the club relocated to Brookhaven and hired Robert Trent Jones, the designer of the Peachtree Golf Club, to build their golf course. For many years, it was the only private club where Jews could play golf in Atlanta.

But by the mid-twentieth century, a proliferation of public courses had brought greater access to the game—and a new cadre of players. Atlanta, in fact, was the site of the first Public Links Tournament, which was held at North Fulton Golf Course in 1948. While less exclusionary than the private clubs, public courses still did not welcome African American players. Late-nineteenth and early-twentieth century white leadership throughout the nation, and especially in the South, supported the concept and goals of racial segregation and utilized means both legal and extralegal, formal and informal, to establish separate facilities, public spaces, and neighborhoods for black citizens. Bobby Jones's hometown was no exception. Policy towards African American use of parks and recreational facilities in Atlanta evolved from restricted usage in the late-nineteenth century to exclusion and the construction of separate parks and facilities by the twentieth century. By 1926, whites had twenty-one playgrounds in Atlanta; blacks had three. By 1932, white Atlantans could choose among sixty-two tennis courts, five golf courses, twelve basketball fields, and one indoor basketball court. African Americans had access to none.

With no city-sponsored options for recreation in sight, Atlanta's African Americans did as had Atlanta's Jews before them—they created their own. The first black club in the South was the Lincoln Country Club, founded in Atlanta in 1927 and formally chartered three years

The female equivalent of the Masters, the Titleholders attracted the nation's best amateur and professional golfers for three decades. *Martha Daniel Papers (MSS-959), Atlanta History Center*

later by Alonzo Fisher, James Ivey, Theodore Grimes, and A. W. Parks. This thirty-three-acre course, on the site of a black cemetery, became a training ground for African American golfers throughout the region. Lincoln was more than a golf course; it also operated as a social club. Unlike many other country clubs of the time, it was also open to women, who could purchase golfing memberships (twelve dollars) as well as social memberships (six dollars). Though Lincoln Country Club filled a very obvious gap and offered African American golfers in Atlanta and surrounding areas a venue in which to play and improve their game, it did have some notable deficiencies. The course consisted of only nine holes, none longer than three hundred yards—compared to four hundred yards on the average course of the period. The greens were small, the course was not professionally maintained, and the clubhouse was but a simple cement block structure. Increasingly dissatisfied with the conditions, some of the golfers—including Dr. Hamilton Holmes, his sons, Alfred "Tup" and Oliver Wendell, and Charles T. Bell—urged the Lincoln Country Club Board of Directors to install an irrigation system. The board refused, accused Dr. Holmes (himself a board member) of disloyalty, and asked him to resign his position. It was then that these four brave men, frustrated over their own home course, tried to gain entrance to the city's whites-only golf course.

The time was right for such action. From the 1940s onward, overt racial segregation in other American sports had slowly begun to dissipate. Baseball was desegregated on April 9, 1947, when Branch Rickey, the general manager of the Brooklyn Dodgers, purchased Jackie Robinson's contract from the Montreal Royals. In 1948, Althea Gibson became the first black woman to play in a national tennis tourna-

The Titleholders was one of the most prestigious events in women's golf. Louise Suggs added a star to her tournament jacket each time she won the event (1946, 1954, 1956, and 1959). *Louise Suggs; William F. Hull, photographer*

ment; just two years later she broke another barrier when she became the first black female golfer to play in a USGA-sponsored event. That same year, in 1950, Earl Lloyd, Chuck Cooper, and Nathaniel "Sweetwater" Clifton joined the National Basketball Association.

On July 19, 1951, Dr. Holmes and the other golfers arrived at the Bobby Jones Golf Course, a public course opened in Atlanta in 1932, "ready, willing, and able to pay all lawful and uniform fees." They were refused admittance by Bill Wilson, the course's manager, who cited a city ordinance that prohibited African Americans from using the park. Later, Charles T. Bell recalled Wilson's polite but firm words, "I am sorry. Negroes cannot play here." The men organized an "Atlanta Golf Committee," and the services of Roscoe Edwin Thomas were retained to file a suit against the city. Thus began a legal battle that would forever change the way golf was played in the United States. Using the

Fourteenth Amendment and *Brown v. Board of Education* as precedents, the litigants won a series of court battles that culminated in a 1955 U.S. Supreme Court decision upholding the Fifth District court ruling that ordered Mayor William B. Hartsfield to desegregate the city's municipal golf courses. (It would not be until 1961 that the Professional Golfers Association would repeal the "Caucasian Race" clause, paving the way for Charlie Sifford to become the first black player to join the PGA Tour.) On December 24, 1955, five African American golfers teed off at Atlanta's North Fulton Course. In 1983, the Atlanta City Council paid tribute to this civil rights struggle by renaming Adams Park the Alfred "Tup" Holmes Memorial Golf Course.

Ironically, professional players—the backbone of today's golfing industry—were once treated as much like second-class citizens in the sport as were blacks and other minority groups. Prior to World War II, tournament organizers made clear distinctions between the "gentlemen" (amateurs) and the "players" (professionals). In 1930, the U.S. Open program bestowed amateurs with the title of "Mr." but denied it to the professional competitors. This snobbery was largely because of the professional players' working-class backgrounds: Walter Hagen was the son of a blacksmith; Sam Snead was the son of a West Virginia farmer; and Gene Sarazen was the son of recent Italian immigrants.

The professionals had first organized themselves in 1916 (as the Professional Golfer's Association, or PGA), but their fledgling tour could not compete with the amateur circuit dominated by players like Bobby Jones. Only a handful of professional players gained national recognition, and they did not become respected competitors until a decade after Jones's

1948 Ladies Golf Union Medal won by Louise Suggs at the British Women's Amateur. *Louise Suggs; William F. Hull, photographer*

retirement. Walter Hagen was the one exception. A former caddie, Hagen successfully challenged country clubs' exclusion of professional players from locker rooms and other amenities and brought about what sportswriters have termed a "social revolution in American golf."

To raise money for the Atlanta Girls Club, Babe Zaharias joined three of Georgia's most famous female golfers in an exhibition match. *Golf subject file, Atlanta History Center*

But the real revolution came later. During the Depression, golf had waned in popularity, largely because of Jones's absence. Professional players had to struggle to support themselves through tournaments, sponsorship, and exhibitions. After World War II, however, and with the advent of television and televised tournaments, professional golf finally caught the public's attention. Professional players—and golf legends—including Byron Nelson, Ben Hogan, Sam Snead, and Arnold Palmer dominated the next two decades.

Television radically altered golf in other ways as well, as sports historian Benjamin Rader attests. The money generated by TV advertising revenues expanded tournament purses. It provoked the touring professionals to break from the PGA and its membership base of mostly club professionals, finally resulting in a separate Tournament Players Division (now the PGA Tour) with its own commissioner. This new player-controlled division has since become responsible for the sport's major tournaments, some of the most prestigious of which have been hosted by Bobby Jones's home club (the Atlanta Athletic Club) and home course (the East Lake Golf Club), including the Ryder Cup (1963) and the PGA Championship (1981 and 1998). Jones himself helped the Atlanta Athletic Club secure the 1976 U.S. Open before his death. On November 16, 1971, he wrote to Robert Howse of the United States Golf Association requesting the "privilege of entertaining the USGA Open Championship," Jones's favorite tournament. Thirty-one days later, Jones died in Atlanta. Eugene Branch, Jones's former law partner, remembered this as one of the last letters Jones wrote. The USGA granted the request, and the Athletic Club opened their Bobby Jones Memorial Room in time for the tournament. Watts Gunn, Jones's fellow competitor and club member, noted that "[t]he only reason they brought the Open here was because of Bobby Jones."

Professional golf for women was an equally tenuous business in the sport's early years. With a limited professional circuit and a ban on playing in amateur events, Hope Seignious organized the Women's Professional Golf Association (WPGA) in 1944, which, in its early years, was composed of a series of contests usually played for one hundred dollar war bonds. To supplement the small purses, most golfers played in exhibitions, offered clinics, and sought sporting goods endorsements. In 1946, Seignious convinced the Spokane Athletic Round Table to donate nineteen thousand dollars for the first U.S. Women's Open, but the WPGA "tour" remained confined to municipal courses and had little public success—until the popular Olympic track star Babe Zaharias took up golf and joined the tour in 1949. The WPGA disbanded that same year, and was replaced by the Ladies Professional Golf Association (LPGA), founded in 1950 by twelve golfers, including Georgian Louise Suggs. As an amateur, Suggs won dozens of major tournaments, including the U.S. Amateur in 1947 and the British Amateur in 1948. As a professional, she won more than fifty LPGA titles.

The most famous women's golf tournament of this period was the Titleholders, founded in Georgia by Dorothy J.

Manice. The first tournament was played in 1937 and was conceived as an annual golf competition among the year's titled champions, amateur and professional. For three decades, the tournament was played at Augusta Country Club and was considered the female counterpart to the Masters. Patty Berg won the first three championships. Other multiple winners include Louise Suggs, Dorothy Kirby, Babe Zaharias, Mickey Wright, Marilynn Smith, and Kathy Whitworth. By 1942,

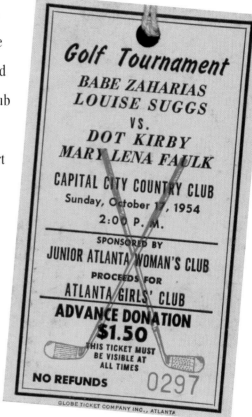

Players badge.
Golf subject file,
Atlanta History Center

the Titleholders Championship had become the oldest seventy-two-hole medal play championship for women held in the United States. After suspending play during World War II, in 1948 the Titleholders became one of the first women's events to offer prize money to female professionals. Similar to the Masters, professionals and selected amateurs were notified by invitation, and each

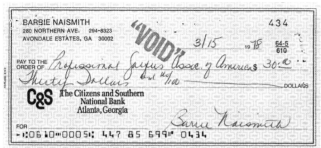

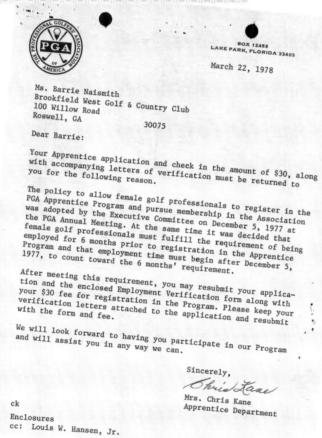

When Barrie Naismith applied for PGA apprentice membership, the PGA voided this check, which prompted her to sue for employment discrimination. *Barrie Naismith Jeffcoat Papers, Atlanta History Center*

Naismith's courage to challenge the PGA's employment practices forever changed professional golf. *Barrie Naismith Jeffcoat Papers, Atlanta History Center*

year's winner was awarded a prized green jacket, sometimes by Bobby Jones. The tournament's increasing cost ended the competition in 1966, with the exception of a brief revival hosted by Peggy Kirk Bell in Southern Pines, North Carolina, in 1972. Eileen Stulb, a two-time Georgia state amateur and member of Augusta Country Club since 1939, was instrumental in a second revival of the Titleholders in 1990.

In the last three decades, two additional events in Jones's home state have helped golf become more inclusive. Although the first event did not make too many headlines, it has had a lasting impact on the game. On March 15, 1978, Barrie Naismith, a female assistant golf professional at Brookfield West Golf and Country Club in Atlanta, applied for and was denied membership as a teaching professional to the PGA. She appealed to the Georgia Section of the PGA and was told by one official that she could "call Jimmy Carter, but it won't do you any good." On May 3, 1978, Naismith hired Atlanta attorney Lawrence Ashe and filed a class-action employment discrimination suit to join the PGA's teaching professionals division, so as to enjoy the same employment opportunities as her male teaching counterparts. (She was not seeking access to the Tournament Players Division; female touring pros were then, as now, governed by the LPGA.) The case was settled out of court, and Naismith was accepted as a Class A member, thus paving the way for female golf professionals throughout the nation to join the PGA as club professionals.

The second event was enacted on a more public stage. In 1997, twenty-one-year-old Tiger Woods became the first African American and the youngest player ever to win the Masters, the tournament founded by Bobby Jones and Clifford Roberts. Woods learned to play on a municipal course in Los Angeles, won three straight U.S. Amateur Championships, and left Stanford University to turn pro in 1996. By the end of the year, he had won two PGA Tour victories, followed by his April 1997 victory in Augusta—18 under par and 12 shots ahead of the second-place finishers. His win was no small accomplishment on a course where club cofounder Roberts once declared: "As long as I'm alive golfers will be white, and caddies will be black."

Just as Jones was the symbol of the amateur era, Woods has become the symbol of golf's modern era. Although he was preceded by a variety of pioneers— Charlie Sifford, who became the first African American to play on the PGA Tour; Lee Elder, who broke the color barrier at the Masters; and Ann Gregory, who became the first African American woman to play in a USGA event—Woods's victory has focused attention on a sport

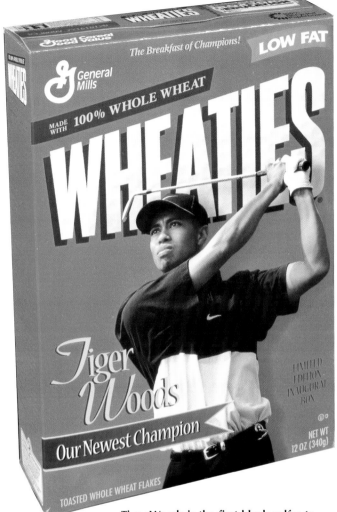

Tiger Woods is the first black golfer to appear on the famous Wheaties box.
General Mills; William F. Hull, photographer

that fifty years ago was largely limited to elite country clubs. Hugh B. Price, president of the National Urban League, declared that Woods's " . . . sheer presence in golf will encourage generations of young people of color to go into this sport." It is fair to say that Woods, like Bobby Jones, has helped make golf the game it is today. ■

Black golfers, prohibited from playing in the PGA events by the "Caucasian Race" clause, formed their own umbrella organization, the United Golfers Association. Atlanta golfers Zeak Hartsfield (left) and Howard Wheeler (third from left) are pictured with Eddie Mallory (second from left) and boxer Joe Louis (right) at Coffin Golf Club in Indianapolis in 1948. *Thomas Smith Photograph Collection (VIS-71f), Atlanta History Center*

Alfred "Tup" Holmes was a distinguished amateur golfer in the 1930s who won three Southern Intercollegiate Athletic Conference championships and three Southern Amateur championships while a student at Tuskegee University.
Holmes Family

Dr. Hamilton Holmes was an Atlanta physician who played on the
United Golfers Association tour, the black equivalent of the PGA.
Holmes Family

Alfred "Tup," Hamilton, and Oliver Wendell Holmes became the first litigants to use *Brown v. Board of Education* as a precedent. *Holmes Family*

Charles T. Bell, shown here with Dr. Catherine Lewis and Charlie Yates at the opening of
Playing Through: African American Golf in Georgia, is one of the original (and the only living)
litigants in the golf course desegregation suit.
Atlanta History Center; William F. Hull, photographer

Geo. Sargent ~ 1909

George Sargent won the 1909 U.S. Open, but is better known as a PGA president (1921–1926)
and head professional at the Atlanta Athletic Club's East Lake Golf Course.
Sargent Family

In 1947, Harold Sargent succeeded his father as head professional at East Lake, and in 1958 he succeded him as
PGA president (1958–1960). They were the only father-son combination to have held this post in PGA history.
He also was instrumental in bringing the 1963 Ryder Cup Matches to East Lake.
Sargent Family

Jack Sargent, who succeeded his brother Harold as golf professional
at East Lake, is shown here with Arnold Palmer.
Sargent Family

Dorothy Kirby began playing golf at age eleven, but did not become a serious golfer until she came under the tutelage of Howard Beckett at the Capital City Club.
Mrs. O.B. Keeler Photographs (VIS-72), Atlanta History Center

Alice Bauer pointing to her name
on the Titleholders scoreboard.
*Kenneth G. Rogers Photograph Collection
(COL-18-16), Atlanta History Center*

NAME																		
ARMSTRONG OAKLAND CALIF.	6	4			4	3			5		3	4		5	3		3	4
ARMSTRONG	4	6	4		4	4	4		49		6	3		3	5			
ARMSTRONG	4	5	5	4	4	4		49		5	6	3		3	4			
ARMSTRONG	5	5	6	3	6	5	8	6	5	37	5	6	3	5	3	5	4	
A ARMSTRONG	5	5	4	3	5	3	3	4	5	36	4	6	3	5	3	5	4	
...ER SARASOTA FLA	4	4	4	4	4	4	4	4	4	36	4	6	3	4	4	4	5	
...ER	5	4	3	5	3	5	5	4	39	4	5	3	4	4	5	5		
...ER	5	5	4	3	5	4	4	5	5	40	5	5	2	4	3	5		
...ER	5	5	4	3	5	4	4	4	7	4	40				3	5	5	
BAU...	6	4	4	3	4				4	5	4	5	3	5	5			
BAUER	6	4	6	3	4	3	5	5	5	41	4	5	4	4	4	6	4	
BAUER	4	4	5	3	4	4	3	5	4	36	6	5	5	3	5			
BAUER ...NES N.C.	4	4	5	3	4	3	4	4	36	5	5	3	4	3	5			
KIRK...	5	5	4	3	4				4	5	3	5	3	5				
Y KI...									5	4	5	3	5	3	5			
	5	5	5	4	5	4	4	5	41	4	5	3	5					
...ST ANDREWS ILL.	4	4	5	4	3	4	6	4	38	4	6	3	4	4	5	3		
	5	4	4	4	4	4	4	4	36	4	5	4	4					
	5	4	4	3	4	4	4	4	39									
...RG							4	4	5	5	3	5	2	5				
...RG	5	6	5	4	6	3	4	6	5	44	5	5	8	3	4	3	6	
...RIE BURNS GREENSBORO N.C.	5	4	5	4	5	4	4	5	40	4	8	3	4	3	6			
...RJORIE BURNS	5	4	5	4	4	4	4	5	40	4	5	3	5	4	6			
...RJORIE BURNS	6	4	5	4	4	4	4	4	5	40								

Bobby Jones presenting Louise Suggs with one of her four Titleholders trophies.
Kenneth G. Rogers Photograph Collection (COL-18-15), Atlanta History Center

Pictured at the 1937 Georgia Women's Amateur Championship at Coosa Country Club in Rome are
Dorothy Kirby, Mrs. Guy Butler (the runner-up), and Martha Daniel (the winner).
Martha Daniel Photographs (MSS-959), Atlanta History Center

Bobby Jones and Louise Suggs, February 1948, the year Suggs won the British Women's Amateur. Two years later, Suggs would help found the LPGA.
Atlanta Journal-Constitution

Bobby Jones giving Dorothy Kirby a photograph of Kirby and her teacher Howard Beckett (head professional at the Capital City Club) on December 5, 1951, after she won the U.S. Women's Amateur.
Atlanta Journal-Constitution

In 1983, the city of Atlanta renamed Adams Park the Alfred "Tup" Holmes Golf Course to recognize an important civil rights struggle.
Holmes Family

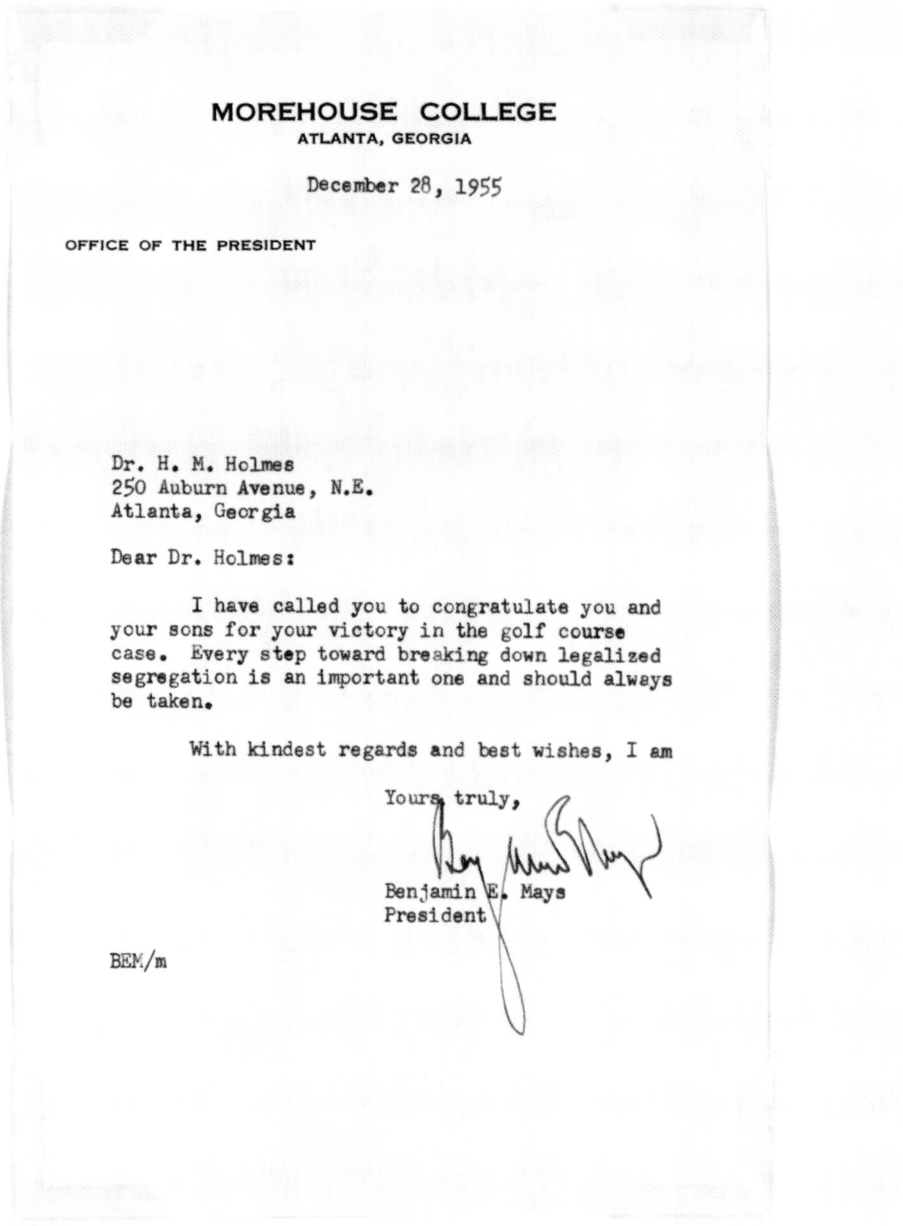

MOREHOUSE COLLEGE
ATLANTA, GEORGIA

December 28, 1955

OFFICE OF THE PRESIDENT

Dr. H. M. Holmes
250 Auburn Avenue, N.E.
Atlanta, Georgia

Dear Dr. Holmes:

      I have called you to congratulate you and
your sons for your victory in the golf course
case. Every step toward breaking down legalized
segregation is an important one and should always
be taken.

      With kindest regards and best wishes, I am

           Yours, truly,

           Benjamin E. Mays
           President

BEM/m

**Benjamin E. Mays, then president of Morehouse College, was one of the many who congratulated
the Holmeses on the successful desegregation suit.**
Holmes Family

The Holmes family at the opening of *Playing Through: African American Golf in Georgia*, a traveling exhibition prepared by the Atlanta History Center for the East Lake Community Foundation, September 11, 1998.
Atlanta History Center; Catherine Lewis, photographer

In 1958, Jones became the second American awarded the Freedom of the City of St. Andrews.
Special Collections Department, Robert W. Woodruff Library, Emory University

DOWN THE FAIRWAY WITH
Bobby Jones

1902
Jones born
March 17

1908
Jones competes in first
tournament, East Lake
Golf Course

1916
Jones wins Georgia State
Amateur Championship;
youngest player
to participate in
U.S. Amateur

1922
Jones completes B.S.
at Georgia Institute
of Technology

1923
Jones wins
first major
tournament,
U.S. Open

1924
Jones receives
English degree
from Harvard;
marries Mary
Rice Malone

1926
Jones becomes
first player
to win both
the U.S. Open
and British Open

1928
Jones admitted to
Georgia Bar
after only one
year of law school

1930
Jones wins
"Grand
Slam,"
retires
from sport

1934
First Masters
played at
Augusta National
Golf Club

1942
Jones serves
as captain in the
Army Air Force

1900   **1910**   **1920**   **1930**   **1940**

CHAPTER 5

MATCHLESS IN SKILL AND CHIVALROUS IN SPIRIT: BOBBY JONES'S LEGACY

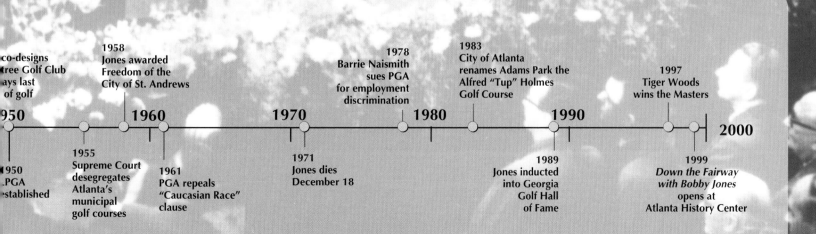

"Perhaps it is best simply to say that there was a touch of poetry to his golf, so there was always a certain, definite magic about the man himself." **HERBERT WARREN WIND**

There is no question that Bobby Jones is one of the best golfers ever to play the game. He won thirteen of the twenty-seven national tournaments he entered, captured the Grand Slam, and helped establish the most famous golf course and tournament in the world. His extraordinary record, though, is not his greatest contribution. Jones recognized that athletic achievements were always less important than character. A poem by Grantland Rice that hung in Jones's Atlanta law office reflected this philosophy: "When the One Great Scorer comes to write against your name, he marks not that you won or lost, but how you played the game." In 1966, Jones reflected in an article for the *Atlanta Journal* that "[t]he quality of sportsmanship is the quality I would most want to be praised for." Reaching this goal, though, was his greatest challenge—and his most enduring legacy.

As a young golfer, Jones was a skillful and aggressive player, but had difficulty controlling his temper. Journalists of the period, including the *Atlanta Journal*'s own O. B. Keeler, worried that Jones's lack of maturity would overshadow his tremendous physical skill.

Grantland Rice described Jones as "a short, rotund kid with the face of an angel and the temper of a timber wolf." Alexa Stirling, Jones's fellow club member and Georgia's first national champion, was forbidden by her father to play with him as a teenager because of his conduct. While barnstorming around the country with Perry Adair, Elaine Rosenthal, and Stirling to raise money for the Red Cross's war effort, Jones recognized that his tantrums were becoming a source of embarrassment. At Brae Burn Country Club, a sportswriter remarked on Jones's performance:

Some interesting golf was shown during the match, interspersed with some pranks by Jones, which will have to be corrected if this player expects to rank with the best in the country. Although Jones is only a boy, his display of temper when things went wrong did not appeal to the gallery.

But rather than improve, Jones's temper tantrums only got worse. In the 1921 British Open at St. Andrews it came to a head.

The historical record is filled with inconsistencies about what actually happened on June 25, 1921, during the third round of the British Open. What we do know is that Jones teed off on a windy morning and shot a 46 on the front nine. He took a double-bogey on the tenth hole (which after his death would be renamed in his memory). But instead of facing another 6 on the par-3 eleventh hole, he pocketed his ball, and thus disqualified himself from the tournament. While some historians have claimed that he then stormed off the course, he in fact continued playing and shot a 72 for the fourth round. Some golf historians, including Geoffrey Cousins, Tom Scott, and Dick Miller, have even suggested that he tore up his scorecard, although it is unlikely. Six years after the incident Jones reflected on it in *Down the Fairway*:

I have some sterling regrets in golf. This is the principal regret—that ever I quit in a competition . . . But I was a youngster, still making my reputation. And I often have wished I could in some way offer a general apology for picking up my ball on the eleventh green of the third round, when I had a short putt left for a horrid 6. It means nothing to the world of golf. But it means something to me.

His reprimand at the British Open did little to change his ways. At the U.S. Amateur later that year in St. Louis, Jones threw a golf club after a bad shot and hit a woman on the leg. Jones lost the hole and the match—and almost lost his amateur career. United States Golf Association President George Walker warned Jones in a letter, "you will never play in a USGA event again unless you can learn to control your temper." Jones returned to Atlanta to ponder his future, aware that he had to change his approach to golf to continue playing the game he loved.

This caricature is one of the few images that parodies Jones's temper. *Sidney L. Matthew*

Over the next several years, Jones's conduct continued to draw national attention—but for a different reason. He called penalty strokes against himself for relatively minor infractions in four national tournaments, often costing himself the championship. The most famous incident of this occurred on the eleventh hole of the 1925 U.S. Open in Worcester, Massachusetts. Jones touched the grass behind the ball with his club, and, although there were no witnesses, he assessed a stroke. This decision prevented him from becoming the only golfer ever to win five U.S. Opens. When the press praised his uncompromising adherence to the rules, he responded, "There is only one way to play the game. You might as well praise a man for not robbing a bank." Gene Sarazen later described this incident as "the greatest display of sportsmanship I've ever witnessed." In less than five years, Jones came to embody the honesty and integrity inherent in the sport and set the standard by which athletes are measured.

Jones's transformation was so complete that the year he won the Grand Slam he was given the Sullivan Award for his promotion of amateur sports by the Amateur Athletic Union of the United States, an organization founded in 1888. Twenty-five years later, the United States Golf Association established the Bob Jones Award, honoring a person who, by a single act or over the years, emulates Jones's

Spalding hired Jones to help design their first matched set of golf clubs.
Sidney L. Matthew;
William F. Hull,
photographer

sportsmanship, respect for the game and its rules, generosity of spirit, sense of fair play, and perhaps even sacrifice. Francis Ouimet was the first recipient, and in 1980, Charlie Yates, Jones's protégé and fellow club member, became the first Georgia player to be given this award. It remains the highest honor in amateur or professional golf.

On October 9, 1958, the city of St. Andrews also honored Jones's contributions to the game of golf by presenting him the Freedom of the City and Royal Burgh of St. Andrews, Scotland. St. Andrews played an important role in Bobby Jones's life and career. It is the place where he harnessed his temper and won the first leg of the Grand Slam. Jones, who once declared that "St. Andrews is the most fascinating golf course I have ever played," modeled both Augusta National and Peachtree Golf Club on the famous Old Course. St. Andrews was also the city that embraced Jones as "our Bobby" after he won the 1927 British Open. Upon receiving the cup, Jones told the crowd that "nothing would make me happier than to take home your trophy. But I cannot. Please honor me by allowing it to be kept here at the Royal and Ancient Club where it belongs." The city's affection was returned when Jones stopped at St. Andrews to play golf in 1936 on his way to Berlin for the Olympic Games. Several hours after he signed his name for a tee time, two thousand Scots gathered on the course to watch Jones play.

The privileges of a Burgess and Guild Brothere included the right to cart shells, take divots, and dry one's washing upon the first and last fairways. While these might seem "homely terms," they indicated that Jones was "free to feel at home at St. Andrews as truly as in his own home of Atlanta." Jones was the second American ever to receive this award, preceded only by Benjamin Franklin in 1759. Upon presentation of the casket and scroll, Lord Provost Robert Leonard (the city's equivalent of mayor) said of Jones:

We welcome him for his own sake; we welcome him also as an ambassador in the cause of international under-standing and good will which the competition of this week is designed to promote. We welcome him, more-over, not only as a distinguished golfer, but as a man of outstanding character, courage, and accomplishment, well worthy to adorn the roll of our honorary burgesses.

In response to the honor, Jones graciously remarked, "I could take out of my life everything except my experiences at St. Andrews and I would still have had a rich and full life." Upon his departure, the entire crowd at Younger Hall sang the Scottish tune "Will Ye No Come Back Again?" with the sad knowledge that he never would. A year after his death, the Royal and Ancient Golf Club named the tenth hole on the Old Course in Jones's memory.

A more recent tribute to Bobby Jones has come from his home-town of Atlanta. In 1998, Charlie Yates and John Imlay Jr., worried about the condition of Jones's gravesite in Oakland Cemetery, turned to the nonprofit Imlay Foundation to refurbish the site. The foundation hired a landscaping team to plant a horseshoe of the same eighteen flowering trees that grace Augusta National's eighteen holes. The gravesite itself is surrounded by pink fairy roses, as well as golf balls and tees left by fans of the nation's most famous golfer.

Jones's legacy as a teacher has endured as well. Years after his death, Sybervision recognized the value of the *How I Play Golf* film series that was originally produced by Warner Brothers in the 1930s and re-released the films on video. Jones's uncomplicated and pragmatic approach to every aspect of

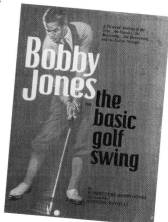

Jones published dozens of arti-cles and four books on golf. His autobiography, *Down the Fairway* (1927) was followed by *Golf Is My Game* (1960), *Bobby Jones on Golf* (1966), and *Bobby Jones: The Basic Golf Swing* (1969). *Robert Tyre Jones Jr. Book Collection, Atlanta History Center; William F. Hull, photographer*

the game has stood the test of time, even with the advent of new equipment and modern golf course architecture. In recent years, Sidney L. Matthew has edited texts on Jones's instruction, including *Secrets of the Master*, and in 1998, Martin Davis of American Golfer published *Classic Instruction*. The book featured never-before-published photographs and instructional notes written by Jones in 1993, along with photographs and commentary by Ben Crenshaw. The United States Postal Service has even honored Jones—twice. In 1981, a decade after his death, a commemorative stamp was issued. And, thanks to the efforts of biographer and collector Sidney Matthew, the Postal Service released a second stamp in 1998 as part of their "Celebrate the Century" series.

Jones's legacy, though, transcends golf. Ben Hogan once remarked that the "secret of Jones's success" was the "strength of the man's mind." He was widely respected for his intellect, particularly in the practice of law. The Robert Tyre Jones Jr. Memorial Lecture on Legal Ethics at Emory University was inaugurated in 1974 by Justice Harry A. Blackmun of the United States Supreme Court and with the support of Jones's for-

The Gorham statue, the only known copy in existence, was displayed in Whitehall Estates, Jones's home on Tuxedo Road. It was featured in the Smithsonian exhibition, *Heroes of American Sports*, in 1981–1982. *1995.14 .M1, Atlanta History Center; William F. Hull, photographer*

mer law firm. An esteemed group participated in this series during its decade-long existence, including Harry A. Blackmun, "Thoughts About Ethics" (1974–75); Professor Paul A. Freund, "The Moral Education of the Lawyer" (1976–77); and Alistair Cooke, "Ethics, Manners and Sportsmanship" (1977–78). Two years after this series began, the Robert T. Jones Jr. Scholarship Program was established by Emory University in Atlanta and the University of St. Andrews in Scotland as an exchange program to nurture college students who "possess the finest academic and personal qualifications." Each year, eight Jones Scholars are selected, four at each university. In addition, two or three graduate students from St. Andrews are offered an opportunity to study at an American university of their choice. The year-long scholarships, funded through three endowments, are intended to help foster the transatlantic ties that were so important to Jones. A Canadian Jones Scholarship Trust also makes a similar exchange.

In 1978, Jones's hometown of Atlanta honored him with the Shining Light Award, created in 1963 by Atlanta's WSB

TV-Radio and Atlanta Gas Light Company to honor those who have made significant contributions to the city. Jones's daughter, Clara Jones Black, accepted the posthumous award to the "supreme personification of amateur sports." Joining fellow honorees Margaret Mitchell and Robert W. Woodruff, a permanent gas light and plaque was placed in Buckhead Park as a tribute to Jones.

While Jones has been inducted into half a dozen athletic and golf halls of fame, museums and private golf clubs throughout the United States and Britain have played a critical role in preserving his legacy. Golf House, opened in 1972 at the headquarters of the United States Golf Association in Far Hills, New Jersey, has a Bob Jones Room that documents his stunning career and features thirty-two tournament medals, a photographic history of the Grand Slam, manuscripts, and his famous putter Calamity Jane II, which is mounted below his portrait. The USGA's photo archives and library also contain materials related to Jones's life. A second Calamity Jane putter is housed at Augusta National Golf Club, which also has a small, but impressive, collection of Jones materials related to his years as a competitor and his longtime relationship to Augusta National and the Masters. The Atlanta Athletic Club's Bobby Jones Memorial Room, opened in time for the 1976 U.S. Open hosted by the club, hosts a diverse collection of Jones's trophies and memorabilia. The club also features an informal archives comprised of manuscripts, photographs, and artifacts related to Jones and his home club. The newly renovated East Lake Golf Course houses an important collection of Jones artifacts and golfing memorabilia from the Golden Age of American Sports, the majority of which is on loan from Jones biographer and collector Sidney L. Matthew. The World Golf Hall of Fame in St. Augustine, Florida, opened in May 1998, features Jones in the seventh hole of their exhibition, titled "A Golden Era." The eighteen-hole installation is one of the most complete presentations of the history of golf in America. The

Jones was presented with this silver casket and scroll at the 1958 ceremony. *Robert Tyre Jones Jr. Collection (1995.14. M1-M2), Atlanta History Center; William F. Hull, photographer*

In 1959, Coca-Cola's Robert W. Woodruff presented Jones this cigarette box with his close friends engraved on the top. *1995.14.M4, Atlanta History Center; William F. Hull, photographer*

British Golf Museum in St. Andrews, Scotland, also documents the history of Jones's amateur career in an installation on five hundred years of golf history. The Special Collections Department at the Robert W. Woodruff Library of Emory University has a large Bobby Jones manuscript collection that contains letters, news clippings, plaques, and photographs. A small case of artifacts documenting Jones, one of the university's most famous students, is on display in the library's reading room.

The most comprehensive exhibition on Jones, though, is at the Atlanta History Center. *Down the Fairway with Bobby Jones*, the only permanent exhibition on Jones in

a public institution, opened on April 5, 1999. The Bob Jones Collection, originally offered for sale by Bobby Jones's grandson, came to the Atlanta History Center in 1994 when a group of local business leaders and foundations joined together to purchase and donate these historic artifacts. Instead of duplicating the efforts of the Georgia Golf Hall of Fame, the United States Golf Association's Golf House, World Golf Village, and the British Golf Museum, *Down the Fairway with Bobby Jones* examines the origins of the game, the growth of specific courses and clubs in the Gilded Age, the rise of public courses, golf course desegregation, the growing professionalization of golf, and the meaning of golf and sport in American culture. Divided into three thematic sections ("The Early History of Golf," "The Age of the Amateur," and "The Making of the Modern Game"), the exhibition strives to contextualize Jones's career within broader themes of sports history.

In addition to the more traditional display, the exhibition also includes a variety of multimedia installations. The introductory video, *Down the Fairway of Time*, explores the origins of the game and the development of the sport during the industrial revolution. It also traces the formation of golf clubs in Georgia from the founding of the

Jones's library is part of the Bob Jones Collection at the Atlanta History Center. *Robert Tyre Jones Jr. Book Collection, Atlanta History Center; William F. Hull, photographer*

and "The Bobby Jones Research Website," a component designed for researchers who are interested in a comprehensive bibliography on Bobby Jones, an illustrated biographical timeline, the founding dates of golf clubs in his home state, and a recordbook of tournaments played in Georgia. This third component also links to related Websites and is available directly via the Internet at www.atlantahistory.net.

Savannah Golf Club (ca. 1794), the nation's second oldest course, to the establishment of the Atlanta Athletic Club's East Lake course where Jones learned to play golf. *A Hero Mightily Esteemed* documents Jones's illustrious playing career with archival footage from his many tournaments. At the end of the third thematic section, visitors are encouraged to explore an interactive kiosk—the most innovative component of the exhibition. This Internet-linked computer station kiosk is divided into three sections: "The Tour of East Lake," a 360-degree tour of Bobby Jones's home course, which allows visitors to view each hole and play the fifteenth hole against Jones; "Classic Instruction," an interactive and animated version of Martin Davis's new book that features beginning and advanced golf instruction from Jones and Ben Crenshaw;

A special issue of *Atlanta History: A Journal of Georgia and the South* devoted entirely to the exhibition was produced in time for the opening of *Down the Fairway with Bobby Jones*. It features three main articles—Sidney L. Matthew's "Atlanta's Immortal Bobby Jones," Dr. Andy Ambrose's " 'Negroes Cannot Play Here': The Desegregation of Atlanta's Golf Courses," and Dr. Catherine Lewis's "The Legacy of Women's Golf in Georgia"—as well as book reviews on Dr. Calvin Sinnette's *Forbidden Fairways: A History of African Americans and the Game of Golf* and Martin Davis's *Classic Instruction*. The journal has become part of the growing canon of scholarship on Jones and golf history. Taken together, the exhibition, Website, journal, and this companion volume have affirmed Bobby Jones's enduring legacy. ■

After his retirement from tournament play, Jones and his wife, Mary, golfed for recreation.
Kenneth G. Rogers Photograph Collection (COL-223-1A), Atlanta History Center

Jones joined his father's law firm in Atlanta after passing the Georgia bar.
Kenneth G. Rogers Photographs (KGR-8-10), Atlanta History Center

Jones, a lieutenant colonel in the Army Air Force during World War II, with (left to right) daughters Mary Ellen and Clara; wife Mary; and son Robert Tyre III.
Dr. and Mrs. William H. Smith Photographs (1993.277), Atlanta History Center

Jones's son, Bob Jones III, played on the Emory Golf Team in 1949.
From left to right are Mickey Baker, Al Shelander, Bob Jones III, Charles "Chuck" Childs, and Coach Johnny Miller.
Charles T. Childs Photograph Collection (1995.215), Atlanta History Center

Jones served as honorary captain of the 1958 World Amateur Team.
United States Golf Association

In 1958, Jones became the second American awarded the Freedom of the City of St. Andrews. *Special Collections Department, Robert W. Woodruff Library, Emory University*

Jones was presented with a two-foot-high bronze sculpture cast by the Gorham Silver Company a year after winning the Grand Slam.
Special Collections Department, Robert W. Woodruff Library, Emory University

"A man never stands so tall as when he stoops to help a boy."
Special Collections Department, Robert W. Woodruff Library, Emory University

Thirteen days after retiring from tournament golf,
Jones signed a contract with Warner Brothers.
*Special Collections Department, Robert W. Woodruff
Library, Emory University*

Jones's close friend, Coca-Cola magnate Robert W. Woodruff, was a visitor to the *How I Play Golf* set.
Special Collections Department, Robert W. Woodruff Library, Emory University

Steel for Backing – about 16"
high by 11" deep by 16" long

Bunker Play

2270-A (1) In playing a full blast or explosive shot from sand, the player faces a little more toward the hole –

2310-A (2) The stance is open – with the right foot advanced (3) and the face of the club is

2306-A laid off, so that its effective loft is increased

1574A (4) but the grip is not altered in any particular.

2309-A (5) The backswing is of ample length and more upright than for the ordinary stroke through the green.

2311-A (6) The club head cuts across the line of play from outside to inside, or from right to left,

2304-A (7) and actually blasts the ball out of the bunker, along with a considerable amount of the sand upon which it is resting.

1558-A-3 (8) This is the safest shot to play in order to make certain of getting out of the bunker,

1594-A (9) when the ball is lying under a high bank.

2298-A (10) When the ball is resting on firm sand and the wall of the bunker is not too high, a clean chip may be attempted.

2300-A (11) When successful, this little shot is a great stroke-saver, but it involves a deal of risk.

2302-A 12. The stroke must be directed downward for if the club strikes the sand before the ball disaster results

---

Putting

1579 (1) In putting, the index finger of the left hand overlaps the little finger of the right, instead of the reverse as in the other strokes.

1576-A-3 (2) Both thumbs are along the top of the shaft so that the two hands are directly opposed.

2284-A (3) The posture at address is one of comfort and complete relaxation. The knees are slightly bent to avoid any feeling of tension in the player's underpinning.

2266-A (4) The feet are close together and the weight about evenly divided between the two. The left elbow is away from the side so that it can move forward without hindrance.

2289-A (5) No attempt is made to "hinge" the stroke upon either the right or left wrist. The arms and shoulders assist in the action and the hips and legs yield to the movement as the need arises.

2259-A (6) To stop or lock the left wrist before or as the club strikes the ball is a serious mistake.

2283-A (7) The backswing brings the club slightly inside the projected line of the putt and the blade is allowed to open naturally.

2285-A (8) The club continues its swing in a flat arc close to the ground and

2271-A (9) finishes in a sweep that is not restricted by taut muscles.

2258-A (10) The little chip, from just off the green, becomes in reality a putt

2257-A (11) when played with a special club of the length and lie of a putter

2256-A (12) but with enough loft to pitch the ball onto the closely cut putting surface.

These photographs and manuscripts were used for an instructional series that Jones produced
after his retirement from tournament play, and were the basis of Martin Davis's *Classic Instruction*.
Robert Tyre Jones Jr. Collection, donated by Anne H. Laird (1998.78), Atlanta History Center

The clubhouse of the Bobby Jones Golf
Course, Atlanta, Georgia, September 1948.
*Courtland F. Luce Jr. Photograph Collection
(LUC-2-2), Atlanta History Center*

Jones played his last round of golf at East Lake in 1948 with Bob Ingram, Tommy Barnes, and Henry Lindner.
Atlanta Athletic Club

An accomplished author and avid reader,
Jones is pictured here in his library.
*Kenneth G. Rogers Photographs
(KGR-241-3), Atlanta History Center*

Jones was an avid sportsman, enjoying trap shooting, horseback riding, tennis, and especially fishing.
Jones Family

Jones and his father, Robert P. Jones (also known as the Colonel)
enjoyed an especially close relationship.
Jones Family

Bob, Bob, and Bob.
Robert Tyre Jones Jr. Visual Arts Collection
(1995.014), Atlanta History Center

**The exhibition's executive committee at the opening of *Down the Fairway with Bobby Jones* (left to right):
Gene McClure, Charlie Yates, Catherine Lewis, John Imlay Jr., Sidney L. Matthew, Rick Beard, Linton Hopkins.**
Atlanta History Center; James E. Fitts, photographer

ABOUT THE ATLANTA HISTORY CENTER

The Atlanta History Center is dedicated to presenting the stories of the South and Atlanta's past, present, and future in a variety of engaging and exciting ways through exhibitions, programs, collections, and research. Through its exploration of Atlanta's history and unique identity, as well as its relationship to the histories of other people and places, the Atlanta History Center operates as a cultural resource for residents and students, as well as a popular attraction for visitors.

The Atlanta Historical Society, a nonprofit organization founded in 1926, runs the Center, which is located in Atlanta's beautiful Buckhead neighborhood. On site is the city's most exciting museum—the Atlanta History Museum, with 30,500 feet of exhibit space. In addition to the museum and its award-winning exhibitions, the Center hosts two historic houses, both of which are listed on the National Register of Historic Places: Swan House, an elegant 1928 mansion, and Tullie Smith Farm, an 1845 plantation-plain house with outbuildings, thirty-three acres of beautiful gardens, and nature trails. Also on site is a research archives with manuscript and photo collections totaling 3.5 million items, as well as a Museum Shop and The Coca-Cola Cafe, a working recreation of a 1950s soda fountain.

ABOUT THE MUSEUM

The Museum tells the story of all Atlanta's people—from Indian settlements to the international city of today—through a series of permanent and temporary exhibitions. Classical details enhance the interior public spaces; the atrium is reminiscent of an early railroad station, evoking Atlanta's beginnings as a transportation center.

Located in the Museum's DuBose Gallery is *Turning Point: The American Civil War*, a dynamic exhibition explaining the critical turning point in U.S. history that established an indivisible nation, ended slavery, and set the United States on a course that would broaden democratic freedoms for all Americans. *Turning Point* features more than fourteen hundred objects from the DuBose Civil War Collection and the Thomas Swift Dickey Civil War Ordnance Collection.

The Goizueta Folklife Gallery is host to *Shaping Traditions: Folk Arts in a Changing South*, which traces the unique and evolving attributes of southern folk culture. Drawing heavily upon the John A. Burrison Folklife Collection, the exhibition features more than five hundred items of handcrafted pottery, woodwork, basketry, weaving, quilting, and metalwork, and explores the lives of several master folk artists.

Metropolitan Frontiers: Atlanta, 1835-2000, traces the city's history from the coming of the railroads and the Civil War to the Civil Rights Movement and the Centennial Olympic Games. This groundbreaking exhibition features hundreds of rare artifacts, antique clothing, historic photographs, video presentations, and special areas for hands-on exploration.

The Museum's newest permanent exhibition is *Down the Fairway with Bobby Jones*, which traces Georgia's incredible golf story, from Augusta National Golf Club and the Masters to the inclusion of women in the game and the integration of public courses. But at the center of it all is the story of the man considered to be the most important golfer in the history of the sport, Robert Tyre "Bobby" Jones Jr. Photographs and personal artifacts tell of his lifelong contribution to the game.

The History Center recruited an executive committee to help guide and finance the project. Led by John P. Imlay Jr., this committee included: Eugene T. Branch, Bobby Jones's former law partner; Dr. Linton Hopkins, author of *Where Bobby Learned to Play*; Gene McClure, former director of the Georgia State Golf Association and a rules official for the United States Golf Association; Sidney L. Matthew, collector and author of *The Life and Times of Bobby Jones*, *The History of Bobby Jones's Clubs*, *Secrets of the Master: The Best of Bobby Jones*, *Bobby Jones on Golf*, and *Champions of East Lake*; and Charlie Yates, 1938 British Amateur Champion and secretary of Augusta National Golf Club. A larger, more diverse forty-member advisory board was also assembled to advise the History Center on issues ranging from the desegregation of Georgia's golf courses to the inclusion of antique golf equipment. The exhibition team sought to involve academic and public historians, collectors, golfers, and educators to reach the broadest possible audience.

ABOUT THE HOUSES

Atlanta's landmark Swan House is an elegant, classically styled mansion. Built in 1928 for the Edward H. Inman Family, heirs to a cotton brokerage fortune, the house was designed by well-known Atlanta architect Philip Trammell Shutze and contains antique and reproduction furnishings original to the home. Swan House shows the lifestyle of a wealthy Atlanta family in the early twentieth century and houses the Philip Trammell Shutze Collection of Decorative Arts.

Tullie Smith Farm is an 1845 plantation-plain farmhouse, moved to the Center from nearby DeKalb County, surrounded by period outbuildings, including an open-hearth kitchen, smokehouse, double corncrib, pioneer log cabin, and barn complete with animals. Tullie Smith Farm interprets rural life in the region before the Civil War.

ABOUT THE GARDENS

Thirty-three acres of beautiful gardens, woodlands, and nature trails at the Atlanta History Center show the horticultural history of the metropolitan Atlanta region.

Gardens include the Mary Howard Gilbert Memorial Quarry Garden, with native plants, wildflowers, bridges, and a stream; the Swan House gardens, featuring formal boxwoods and classical statuary; Swan Woods Trail, labeled for nature study; the Garden for Peace, featuring the Soviet Georgian sculpture "The Peace Tree"; Tullie Smith Farm's traditional vegetable, herb, and flower gardens; the Frank A. Smith Memorial Rhododendron Garden, featuring dozens of species of rhododendrons and azaleas; and the Cherry-Sims Asian-American Garden, featuring species from the southeastern United States and their Asian counterparts.

ABOUT THE ARCHIVES

The archives of the Atlanta History Center houses manuscript, book, and photograph collections related to the history of the city, the state, and the South. A strong emphasis is placed on the people, businesses, organizations, places, and events that have played a role in shaping this history. Other subjects represented in the archives collections are genealogy, decorative arts, folk art, architecture, golf, and African American and Native American history. Researchers and media can also purchase copies of photographs and images from the Center's collections. The Cherokee Garden Library, founded by the Cherokee Garden Club in 1973, offers an extensive gardening and horticulture research collection.

Atlanta History Center
130 West Paces Ferry Road, NW
Atlanta, Georgia 30305-1366
(404) 814-4000
http://www.atlantahistory.net

APPENDIX I
TIMELINE

1902 Robert Tyre "Bobby" Jones Jr. is born on March 17 to Robert P. and Clara Jones in the Atlanta neighborhood of Grant Park.

1908 At age six, Jones competes in his first tournament—the East Lake Children's Tournament. Although technically defeated by Alexa Stirling, he is awarded the trophy.

1916 At age fourteen, Jones wins the Georgia State Amateur Championship, defeating Perry Adair. He also travels to the Merion Cricket Club near Philadelphia to become the youngest competitor in the U.S. Amateur; he loses in the third round to Bob Gardner.

1916-22 During what sportswriter O. B. Keeler labeled the "Seven Lean Years," Jones plays in dozens of tournaments but is unable to capture a major championship.

1917 Jones becomes the youngest player ever to win the Southern Amateur. Jones plays in numerous exhibition events with fellow young golfers Perry Adair, Alexa Stirling, and Elaine Rosenthal, raising more than $150,000 for the American Red Cross World War I relief effort.

1921 On June 25, during the third round of the British Open, Jones loses his temper and disqualifies himself from the tournament. Both Jones and historians mark this as the most "transcendent moment of his golfing career."

1922 Jones, who graduated from Atlanta's Tech High School at sixteen, completes his B.S. in mechanical engineering at the Georgia Institute of Technology.

1923 Jones wins his first major championship, the U.S. Open, at Inwood Country Club in New York. He beats Bobby Cruickshank in a playoff, thus ending the "Seven Lean Years."

1924 Jones wins the U.S. Amateur at the Merion Cricket Club in Ardmore, Pennsylvania, defeating George Von Elm 9 and 8 in the final round.

1924 Jones receives a degree in English literature from Harvard. On June 17 he marries Mary Rice Malone in Atlanta. They eventually have three children: Clara, Robert Tyre Jones III, and Mary Ellen.

1925 Jones wins the U.S. Amateur at Oakmont Country Club in Pennsylvania, defeating fellow East Lake golfer Watts Gunn 8 and 7 on the 29th hole. This is the only time two members of the same club have met in the finals of a major championship.

1926 Jones wins his first British Open at Royal Lytham and St. Annes. He hits what has been called "the greatest shot in the history of British golf" on the 17th hole to pull ahead of American professional Al Watrous. Jones was the first American amateur to win the Open.

1926 Jones becomes the first golfer to win the "double"—the U.S. Open and the British Open—in a single season, by winning the U.S. Open at Scioto Country Club in Columbus, Ohio. He went into the final hole tied with Joe Turnesa, but birdied the hole to win the Open by a stroke.

1927 Jones publishes *Down the Fairway* in collaboration with O. B. Keeler, an *Atlanta Journal* sportswriter and Bobby Jones's "secret weapon."

1927 Jones successfully defends his British Open championship at the Old Course in St. Andrews, Scotland.

1927 Jones wins the U.S. Amateur at the Minikhada Club in Minneapolis, defeating Chick Evans 8 and 7 on the 29th hole of the thirty-six-hole final.

1928 After little more than one year at Emory University Law School, Jones passes the state bar exam. On January 13 he is admitted to the Georgia Bar and enters his father's law firm.

1928 Jones wins his fourth U.S. Amateur by defeating T. Philip Perkins 10 and 9 at the Brae Burn Country Club near Boston.

1929 Jones wins the U.S. Open at Winged Foot Golf Club in Mamaroneck, New York. Going to the 17th hole during the last round, Jones needed two pars just to force a playoff. He got his par and pitched onto the 18th green, leaving him with a difficult putt to tie. He made the putt, forcing a thirty-six-hole playoff with Al Espinoza. He dominated the playoff and defeated Espinoza by 23 strokes.

1930 Jones captains the Walker Cup team, played at the Royal St. George's Golf Club in Sandwich, England. The team went on to win the Cup 10 to 2.

1930 Jones plays in what he terms "the most important tournament of my life"—the 1930 British Amateur at St. Andrews. He defeats Roger Wethered on the 13th hole of the second eighteen to win his first and only British Amateur.

1930 Jones goes to Hoylake, England, to play in the British Open at the Royal Liverpool Golf Club. After the second round, Jones was a stroke ahead. He struggled in the third round and shot a 2-over-par 74. He shot a 75 in the fourth round to hold on for the win.

1930 Shortly after his triumphant return from Britain, Jones heads to the Interlachen Country Club in Minneapolis for the U.S. Open. Jones shot a 1-under-par 71 in the first round to stay one behind the leaders. He finished the second round at 73-even for the tournament and 2 strokes off the lead. He then played an outstanding third round, shooting 68 to give himself a 5-stroke lead going into the fourth, and an erratic fourth round, making three double-bogeys and three birdies on the way to a 3-over-par 75. Jones waited more than an hour while Macdonald Smith, his closest pursuer, finished 2 strokes back, giving Jones his fourth U.S. Open championship.

1930 Jones returns to the Merion Cricket Club, the site of his first U.S. Amateur competition and his first win in the Amateur, to try and complete the Grand Slam of golf. During the finals the Marines were brought out to help control the huge crowds that were grabbing at Jones. He won the medal and the "Impregnable Quadrilateral of Golf," also known as the Grand Slam, in the qualifying round with a record 142.

1930 On November 13 Jones signs a contract with Warner Brothers to make a series of one-reel motion pictures devoted entirely to golf instruction.

1930 On November 17 Bobby Jones announces his retirement from golf.

1932 Augusta National Golf Club, designed by Bobby Jones and Dr. Alister MacKenzie, is completed in December and opens for play the following month.

1934 The First Annual Invitational Tournament, now known as the Masters, is played in March at Augusta National.

1942 On June 9 Jones is commissioned as a captain in the Army Air Force. A medical disability and his age (forty) does not com-

pel him to go to war, but he insists upon serving. He is honorably discharged in August 1944.

1948 Peachtree Golf Club, an Atlanta course designed by Robert Trent Jones and Bobby Jones, opens.

1948 Owing to poor health, Jones plays his last round of golf at East Lake with Bob Ingram, Tommy Barnes, and Henry Lindner.

1955 Jones is diagnosed with syringomyelia, a degenerative spinal disease. That same year the United States Golf Association establishes the annual Bob Jones Award, honoring a person who, by a single act or over the years, emulates Jones's sportsmanship, respect for the game and its rules, generosity of spirit, sense of fair play, self-control, and perhaps even sacrifice. The award's first recipient is Francis Ouimet.

1958 The people of St. Andrews confer the Freedom of the City and the Royal Burgh of St. Andrews on Jones. The only other American ever so honored was Benjamin Franklin in 1759.

1960-69 Jones publishes *Golf is My Game* (1960), *Bobby Jones on Golf* (1966), and *Bobby Jones on the Basic Golf Swing* (1969).

1971 Bobby Jones dies on December 18 and is buried in Atlanta's Oakland Cemetery. On this day, golfers at St. Andrews stopped their play and the flag at the clubhouse was lowered to half-mast.

1972 On July 20 Jones is inducted into the Southern Golf Hall of Fame.

1972 After a memorial service on September 10 at Trinity Church, the 10th hole at the Old Course at St. Andrews is named in honor of Bobby Jones.

1976 Atlanta's Emory University establishes the Bobby Jones Scholarship Program, a scholarship exchange program with St. Andrews University in Scotland.

1981 A commemorative Bobby Jones stamp is issued by the U.S. Postal Service.

1989 On January 14 Bobby Jones is inducted into the Georgia Golf Hall of Fame.

1998 A second commemorative stamp is issued as part of the U.S. Postal Service's "Celebrate the Century" series in 1998.

1999 *Down the Fairway with Bobby Jones*, the only permanent exhibition on Jones's life and legacy, opens at the Atlanta History Center.

APPENDIX II
RESOURCES

Resources (Archives, Museum Collections, Websites) Related to Robert Tyre "Bobby" Jones Jr.

Alston & Bird, LLP
One Atlantic Center
1201 West Peachtree Street
Atlanta, Georgia 30309-3424
(404) 881-7000

The American Golfer
151 Railroad Avenue
Greenwich, Connecticut 06830
(203) 862-9720

Associated Press
Photograph Department
50 Rockefeller Plaza
New York, New York 10020
(212) 621-1500

Atlanta Athletic Club
Bobby Jones Drive
Duluth, Georgia 30136
(770) 448-2166

Atlanta History Center
130 West Paces Ferry Road, NW
Atlanta, Georgia 30305-1366
(404) 814-4000
www.atlantahistory.net

Atlanta Journal-Constitution
72 Marietta Street, NW
Atlanta, Georgia 30303
(404) 526-5420

Augusta National Golf Club
P.O. Box 2086
Augusta, Georgia 30903
(706) 667-6000
www.masters.org

British Golf Museum
The Bruce Embankment
St. Andrews
Fife KY16 9AB
Scotland
1334-478880

Corbis-Bettmann
902 Broadway
New York, New York 10010-6002
(212) 777-6200
www.corbis.com

East Lake Golf Club
2575 Alston Drive, SE
Atlanta, Georgia 30317
(404) 373-5722

Georgia Golf Hall of Fame
One 10th Street
Suite 745
Augusta, Georgia 30901
(706) 724-4443
www.gghf.org

Georgia State Golf Association
121 Village Parkway
Building 3
Marietta, Georgia 30067
(770) 955-4272
www.gsga.org

George Eastman House
900 East Avenue
Rochester, New York 14607-2298
(716) 271-3361

High Museum of Art
1280 Peachtree Street, NE
Atlanta, Georgia 30309
(404) 733-4400

Highlands Country Club
981 Dillard Road
Highlands, North Carolina 28741
(828) 526-2181

Historic Golf Prints
20 Hill Avenue
Fort Walton Beach, Florida 32548
(800) 874-0146

James River Country Club
1500 Country Club Road
Newport News, Virginia 23606
(804) 596-4772

Los Angeles Public Library
630 West Fifth Street
Los Angeles, California 90071
(213) 228-7000

Marietta Museum of History
1 Depot Street
Suite 200
Marietta, Georgia 30060-1901
(770) 528-0431

New York Times
Historic Photograph Archives
299 West 43rd Street
New York, New York 10036
(800) 221-3221

Ralph W. Miller Golf Library
1 Industry Hills Parkway
City of Industry, California 91744
(626) 854-2354

Special Collections
Doheny Memorial Library
University of Southern California
Los Angeles, California 90089-0182
(213) 740-6050

Special Collections Department
Robert W. Woodruff Library
Emory University
Atlanta, Georgia 30322
(404) 727-6887
www.emory.edu/LIB/schome.htm

Tony Stone Images
122 S. Michigan Avenue
Suite 900
Chicago, Illinois 60603
(312) 344-4500

United States Golf Association
Golf House
P.O. Box 708
Far Hills, New Jersey 07931
(908) 234-2300
www.usga.org

University of St. Andrews Library
Photographic Collection
North Street
St. Andrews
Fife KY16 9TR
Scotland
1334-462324

Western Golf Association
1 Briar Road
Golf, Illinois 60029-0301
(847) 724-4600

Winged Foot Golf Club
Fenimore Road
Mamaroneck, New York 10543
(914) 698-8400

World Golf Village
21 World Golf Place
St. Augustine, Florida 32092
1-800-WGV-4746
www.wgv.com

BIBLIOGRAPHY

Alliance Theatre Company (Atlanta, Georgia). "A Tribute to Bobby Jones." Unpublished pamphlet, 1976.

"Amateur Golf Title: Mr. Bobby Jones Crowns His Record." *The Scotsman*, 2 June 1930.

"The American Championship." *American Golfer*, October 1916.

"American Eagles and Birdies." *Outlook*, 30 August 1954, 12.

Anderson, Dave. "Golf's Bobby Jones Revival." *New York Times*, 14 April 1996, 81.

_____. "Methuselah of Masters Rates Personal Bests." *New York Times*, 12 April 1998.

"Anglo-American Golf Final." *The Scotsman*, 31 May 1930.

"Another Jones Triumph." *The Scotsman*, 15 July 1927.

Armour, Tommy. "Pinshots of the Masters." *American Golfer*, October 1935.

"Army Air Corps Captaincy Given To Bobby Jones." *Atlanta Journal*, 9 June 1942.

Aultman, Dick. "An Uncomplicated Approach." *Golf Digest*, April 1989, 164-165.

Bartlett, James Y. "The Golf Bag." *Forbes*, 11 March 1996, 69-74.

Behrand, John. *The Amateur: The Story of the Amateur Golf Championship, 1885-1995.* Worcestershire, Britain: Severnside Printers Ltd., 1995.

Bisher, Furman. "Bobby Jones Revisited." *Atlanta Magazine*, August 1963, 47-53.

_____. "The Gentleman Athlete." *Atlanta Journal*, 20 December 1971, 1D, 8D.

_____. "Golf's Teenage Sensation." *Golf Digest*, April 1965, 30.

_____. "The Southern Gentleman." *Golf Magazine*, September 1960, 58.

Blodgett, Robert. "The King Tees up for the Movies." *Golfers Magazine*, December 1930.

"Bob Jones In Britain But Not To Play Golf." *Atlanta Journal*, 9 January 1944.

"Bob Jones: Many Things to Many People." *Atlanta Journal-Constitution*, 19 December 1971, 3D-4D.

"Bob Jones Ready for Minikhada." *Minneapolis Tribune*, 21 August 1927, 10.

"Obituary: Bobby Jones." *Atlanta Constitution*, 19 December 1971.

"Bobby Jones Achieves His Ambition." *St. Andrews Citizen*, 7 June 1930.

"Bobby Jones, Amateur." *Outlook*, 7 July 1926, 336-337.

"Bobby Jones: America's Unofficial Ambassador." *The City Builder*, July 1930, 5, 6, 9.

"Bobby Applies For Army Discharge." *Atlanta Constitution*, 25 August 1944.

"Bobby Beats Homans For Title as 10,000 Cheer." *Atlanta Journal*, 28 September 1930.

"Bobby Jones Begins Service In Air Corps." *Atlanta Journal*, 24 June 1942.

"Bobby Himself." *The Atlanta Journal*, 14 July 1930.

"Bobby Jones 'Champion Peter Pan': His Book." *The Literary Digest*, 3 September 1927, 38, 40, 44, 46.

"Bobby 'Coasted In' Grantland Rice Says." *Atlanta Constitution*, 25 September 1930, 19.

"Bobby Jones Confides How He Does It." *The Literary Digest*, 31 July 1926, 42-44.

"Bobby Jones Conquers the Golf World." *The Literary Digest*, 30 July 1927, 52-56.

"Bobby Jones and the Duke of Windsor at Augusta, Georgia." *Atlanta Journal-Constitution Magazine*, 18 May 1952.

"Bobby Jones and England." *Living Age*, 7 August 1926, 335

"Bobby Jones' Gesture." *St. Andrews Citizen*, 25 October 1958.

"Bobby Jones' Grand Slam of Golf, I: The British Amateur Championship." *Golf*, August 1965, 24.

"Bobby Jones Grand Slam of Golf, II: The British Open Championship." *Golf*, August 1965, 27.

"Bobby Jones' Grand Slam of Golf, III: The United States Open Championship." *Golf*, August 1965, 29.

"Bobby Jones' Grand Slam of Golf, IV: The United States Amateur Championship." *Golf*, August 1965, 32.

"Bobby Jones: The Greatest Golfer." *The City Builder*, August 1927, 3.

"Bobby Jones In Attendance at Ga-Fla Trials." *Thomasville Times Enterprise*, 17 February 1938.

"Bobby Jones Is Here." *Dundee Courier & Advertiser*, 25 April 1936.

"Bobby Jones' Jeanie Deans." *Golf Digest*, September 1984.

"Bobby Jones Loses at Golf But Wins Affection of Others." *The Literary Digest*, 7 April 1934, 42.

"Bobby Jones Off For California." *Hearst Newspaper*, 18 August 1929.

"Bobby Jones On His Victory." *Dundee Courier & Advertiser*, 2 June 1930.

"Bobby Jones On His Victory." *St. Andrews Citizen*, 2 June 1930.

"Bobby Jones: Only Golfer To Win Grand Slam Dies At 69." *New York Times*, 19 December 1971.

"Bobby Jones Quits Law School and Will Enter Business Here Following Trip to New York." *The Atlanta Constitution*, 3 January 1928, 15.

"Bobby Jones Ready for Charity Match." *Los Angeles Herald Express*, 24 March 1931.

"Bobby Jones Still Idol of St. Andrews." *St. Andrews Citizen*, 11 October 1958.

"Bobby Jones Sues U.S. For Refund in Taxes on Income." *Los Angeles Times*, 6 December 1934.

"Bobby Jones: This Will Come First in My Heart." *Dundee Courier & Advertiser*, 10 October 1958.

"Bobby Jones Upsets Hollywood." *The Literary Digest*, 18 April 1931, 44-45.

"Bobby Jones Will Get Quarter Million for Moving Picture Work." *Atlanta Constitution*, 18 November 1930.

"Bobby Jones Wins British Amateur Golf Crown." *Atlanta Journal*, 31 May 1930, 1.

"Bobby Jones Wins Final Golf Crown of Year." *Montana Standard*, 28 September 1930, 1.

"Bobby Jones Wins Fourth Title of Year, Reaching Ultimate Peak of Golf Glory." *Atlanta Constitution*, 28 September 1930.

"Bobby Jones Won Fame on the Golf Course But He Showed His True Greatness as a Man." *Atlanta Constitution*, 17 March 1954.

"Bobby Jones at Younger Hall: Complete Report of his Speech Momentous and Historic Occasion." *St. Andrews Citizen*, 18 October 1958.

"Bobby Sees Old Course Again." *Dundee Courier & Advertiser*, 4 October 1958.

"Bobby Watching Waistline For Debut In The Movies; Grand Opera Is Pet Music." *Rochester New York Times Union*, 23 February 1931.

Bowden, Ken. "Bobby Jones On Golf." *Golf Digest*, April 1990, 170-80.

Brennan, John M. "Bobby Jones and His Calamity Jane." *Metropolitan Golfer*, March 1952.

"The British Amateur." *U.S.G.A. Golf Journal*, March 1971.

Browning, Robert. *A History of Golf: The Royal and Ancient Game*. London: J. M. Dent, 1955.

Burnes, Robert L. *50 Golden Years of Sports*. St. Louis: Rawlings Manufacturing Company, 1948.

Burnet, Bobby. *The St. Andrews' Opens*. Edinburgh: Sportsprints Pub., 1990.

"Bygone Days." *The Commercial Appeal*, 14 August 1998.

Callaway, Ely. "Searching for Bobby Jones." *Time/Links*, March 1998.

Cantwell, Robert. "The Reel Life of Bobby Jones." *Sports Illustrated*, 23 September 1968.

"A Champion Returns to St. Andrews." *Sports Illustrated*, 20 October 1958, 34.

Clayton, Ward. "Callaway to Help Unveil Bobby Jones Sculpture Tonight." *Augusta Chronicle*, 10 January 1998, B-1.

_____. "The Pre-Masters." *Golf Magazine*, April 1993, 108-109.

Cooke, Alistair. "What Have We Left For Bobby Jones?" *Golf Digest*, April 1996, 121-26.

"Cordial Welcome for Bobby Jones." *St. Andrews Citizen*, 1 August 1936.

Cotton, Henry. *A History of Golf Illustrated*. Philadelphia: Lippincott, 1975.

Cousins, Geoffrey. "Bobby Jones: Infant Prodigy to Golf Colossus." *London Daily Telegraph*, 19 December 1971.

Crawley, Leonard. "Bobby Jones The Master." *The Field*, 16 October 1958, 689.

D.S. "Keeping Up With The Joneses." *Golf and Travel*, Summer 1997, 45.

Dale, Donoval. "Bob's Powder Not Damp, Danforth Says." *Atlanta Constitution*, 11 July 1930, 15.

Dalyrimple, Dolly, "Dolly Interviews Bobby Jones' Boswell." *Birmingham News-Age Herald*, 16 October 1927.

Danzig, Allison and Peter Brandwein. *Sport's Golden Age*. New York: Harper and Brothers, 1948.

Darsie, Darsie L. "Green Tee." *Los Angeles Herald Express*, 15 April 1931.

Darwin, Bernard. "Bobby Jones Worship in England." *Vanity Fair*, July 1930, 70.

_____. *Golf Between Two Wars*. London: Chatto & Windus, 1944.

_____. *Green Memories*. London: Hodder & Stoughton, 1928.

_____. *The Complete Golfer: The Immortal Bobby*. New York: Simon & Schuster, 1954.

Davies, David. "Four Strokes that Shaped Lytham Lore." *Guardian*, 17 July 1996, 23.

_____. "The Jones Story Remains a Fascinating Open Book." *Guardian*, 18 December 1990, 13.

Davis, Bob. "Photobiography." *American Golfer*, June 1935.

Davis, Evangeline. *The Lure of Highlands*. Highlands: Private Publication by Highlands Country Club, 1981.

Davis, Martin. *The Greatest of Them All: The Legend of Bobby Jones*. Greenwich, Conn.: American Golfer, Inc., 1996.

"The Decade: 1928-1937." *Golf Magazine*, January 1988, 46-47.

Dey, Joseph C. Jr. "It Was Always Jones Against the Field." *Golf*, August 1965, 14-15, 73-77.

Dobereiner, Peter. "Congregation of Champions." *Golf Digest*, June 1995, 128-134.

_____. "The Future Was Then." *Golf Digest*, March 1990, 98-103.

"Dogwood, Peaches and a Man Named Jones." *Golf Magazine*, April 1965, 26-8, 33, 36, 38.

Doust, Dudley. "Museum Piece: A Brief History of the World's Most Famous Putter and Its Resurrection." *U.S.G.A. Golf Journal*, 1976.

"Down in Four." *Time*, 22 September 1930.

Dreyspool, Joan Flynn. "Tommy Armour Analyzes The Jones Swing." *Golf*, September 1960.

"A Duffers Consolation." *American Golfer*, February 1931.

Durant, John, ed. *Yesterday in Sports*. New York: A. S. Barnes and Company, 1956, 94-105.

Durant, John, and Otto Bettman. *Pictorial History of American Sports*. New York: A. S. Barnes and Company, 1952, 192-197.

East, J. Victor. "Bobby Jones and His Calamity Jane." *Golf Digest*, May 1962.

"Eben Byers." *U.S.G.A. Golf Journal*, October 1992.

"Eighteen Walker Cup Players Set for Bob Jones Tourney." *The Highlander*, 28 July 1998, 1, 3.

Elliott, Charles. "Bobby Jones Gave Me A Fishing Lesson." *Atlanta Journal*, 11 July 1954.

_____. "Bobby Jones Gave Me A Fishing Lesson." *Atlanta Journal*, 30 September 1930.

_____. "Bobby Jones Gave Me A Fishing Lesson." *Atlanta Journal*, 17 November 1930.

_____. "Bobby Jones Gave Me A Fishing Lesson." *Atlanta Journal*, 15 January 1931.

_____. *East Lake Country Club*. Atlanta: Cherokee Publishing Co., 1984.

_____. *Mr. Anonymous*. Atlanta: Cherokee Publishing Co., 1982.

_____. *An Outdoor Life: The Autobiography of Charlie Elliott*. Atlanta: Flat Rock Press, 1994.

Emory University. "The Robert Tyre Jones Jr. Memorial Lecture on Legal Ethics." Unpublished pamphlets, 1974-1999.

"Epic Putt Replayed." *Life*, 18 October 1954, 49.

Evans, Charles (Chick) Jr., with foreword by Bobby Jones. *Chick Evans Golf Book*. New York: Thos. E. Wilson & Co., 1921.

Falls, Joe. "Jones Spoke With His Sticks." *Detroit News and Free Press*, 7 April 1996, 23.

Farrell, L. A. "Massed Thousands Cheer for Bobby." *The Atlanta Constitution*, 15 July 1930, 1.

Fimrite, Ron. "The Emperor Jones." *Sports Illustrated*, 11 April 1994, 104-16.

Flaherty, Tom. *The Masters*. New York: Holt, Rinehart & Winston, 1961.

_____. *The U.S. Open 1895-1965*. New York: E. P. Dutton & Co., 1966.

"For Masters Only." *Time*, 15 April 1946, 62-63.

Fountain, Charles. *Sportswriter: The Life and Times of Grantland Rice*. New York: Oxford University Press, 1993.

Fraley, Oscar. "Springtime and Bobby Jones." *Golf Magazine*, April 1964, 21-23, 78-79.

Fraser, Alexa Stirling. "The Most Unforgettable Character I've Met." *Reader's Digest*, April 1960, 55-60.

Gallico, Paul. *Farewell to Sport*. New York: Alfred A. Knopf, 1938.

_____. "The Golden People of a Golden Decade." *Chicago Tribune*, 5 April 1964.

_____. "Jones of Jonesville, Georgia." *Liberty*, 26 October 1929.

Ganem, Roger. "The Tools of Victory." *Golf*, August 1965, 38, 58-60.

Gibson, Nevin. *The Encyclopedia of Golf With The Official All-Time Records*. New York: A. S. Barnes, 1958.

"Golden Anniversary of the Grand Slam." *Golf World*, 22 February 1980.

"Golden Jubilee of Golfing Grand Slam." *Dundee Courier & Advertiser*, 16 February 1980.

Golf Magazine (Bobby Jones issue), September 1960.

Golf Magazine (Grand Slam commemorative issue), August 1965.

"Golf's Conquering Hero Home Today." *Atlanta Constitution*, 29 October 1930, 1.

"Golfer of the Golden Era." *Newsweek*, 27 December 1971.

"Golfer of the Half Century." *Golf World*, 3 January 1951.

The Golfer Magazine (Bobby Jones issue), March 1953.

Golfing Magazine Illustrated (Bobby Jones issue), September 1926.

Goodwin, Stephen. "Heroes for the Ages." *Golf Magazine*, December 1997, 48-55.

Gordin, Richard Davis, "Robert Tyre Jones Jr.: His Life and Contributions to Golf." Ph.D. diss., Ohio State University, 1967.

Gould, Alan. "Jones, 287, Wins Open, Mac Smith Second." *Los Angeles Examiner*, 13 July 1930.

Gould, Dave. "Spalding From The Beginning. " *Golf Illustrated*, March 1991.

Graffis, Herb. "The Grand Slam Anniversary Issue." *Golfing*, April 1960.

Green, Kell. *The Golf Swing of Bobby Jones: An Analysis of His Drive*. Chicago: Dixon Press, 1931.

Gregory, C. E. "O. B. Keeler Is Given Watch And Honorary Membership By The Associated Press." *Atlanta Journal*, 19 August 1926.

Griffin, George C. "Bob Jones, Class of 22." *Georgia Tech Alumnus*, Winter 1972.

Grizzard, Lewis. "Letter from Jones Landed the Open." *The Atlanta Journal*, 8 October 1972, 1D.

Gwin, Yolande. "Bobby Jones Room." *Atlanta Journal-Constitution*, 13 June 1976, 3G.

Hanley, Reid. "A Master: Bobby Jones Golf Video." *Chicago Tribune*, 10 March 1989.

Hannigan, Frank. "The Lost Letters of Bobby Jones." *Golf Digest*, April 1994, 108-19, 154-61.

_____. "The Power Broker: From Inventing the Masters to Electing a President, Clifford Roberts Knew How to Pull All the Right Levers." *Golf Digest*, April 1996, 146-210.

Harris, Robert. *Sixty Years of Golf*. London: Batchworth Press, 1953.

Harrison, Dave. "Jones Didn't Feel Ready for U.S. Open, but. . . ." *Augusta (Ga.) Chronicle Herald*, 2 April 1972, 2-3G.

Hornung, Paul. *Scioto CC: 75 Years of History*. City: Scioto Country Club, 1993.

"Hoover Greets Bobby Wishes Him Success In American Amateur." *Atlanta Constitution*, 16 September 1930.

"How Bobby Jones Overcame His Temper." *Liberty*, 7 June 1924, 3.

"How Many More Titles Are In Store For 'Our Bobby'?" *The Literary Digest*, 17 September 1927, 63, 67.

Howard, Jock. "The Man Who Knows More About Bobby Jones Than Any One Else in the World." *Golf World*, April 1998.

"Is Bobby Jones Losing Interest in Golf?" *The Literary Digest*, 21 September 1929, 66-69.

Jackson, Teague. "Flood of Eulogies Pours in for Jones." *Atlanta Constitution*, 19 December 1971.

_____. "Masters Just Not Quite the Same Without Jones." *Atlanta Journal-Constitution*, 9 April 1972, 10D.

_____. "This Summer's U.S. Open Dedicated to Bobby Jones." *Atlanta Journal-Constitution*, 16 March 1969, 12.

Jenkins, Dan. "The Masters: Bobby Jones Started It All." *Sports Illustrated*, 6 April 1978.

_____. "My Lists of Golf's Greatest Moments." *Golf Digest*, July 1996, 40.

"Jones and Ravielli." *Golf Digest*, August 1969.

Jones, Ben Perry. *Robert Tyre Jones: A Family Perspective*. Canton, Ga.: privately printed, 1990.

"The Jones Complex on the Golf Links." *The Literary Digest*, 6 October 1928.

"Jones Explains How To Play Whitfield Course." *Sarasota (Fla.) Herald*, 19 December 1925.

"Jones Graveside Services at Oakland are Private." *Atlanta Journal*, 20 December 1971.

"Jones is Mourned at Scottish Links." *New York Times*, 19 December 1971.

Jones, Paul. "Swinging With Bobby Jones." *Atlanta Constitution*, 1 May 1975, 16.

"Jones Returns to Atlanta on Par with Ben Franklin." *Atlanta Constitution*, 15 October 1958.

Jones, Robert Trent. "Atlanta's New Peachtree Is Pre-Tested by Bobby Jones." *Golfdom*, March 1949, 61-62.

Jones, Robert Tyre Jr. *Bobby Jones on the Basic Golf Swing*. New York: Doubleday, 1969.

_____. *Bobby Jones on Golf*. Garden City, N.Y.: Doubleday and Co., 1966.

_____. *Golf is My Game*. Garden City, N.Y.: Doubleday and Co., 1960.

_____. "Goodbye to Golf." *Liberty*, 31 January 1931.

_____. *How To Run A Golf Tournament*. New York: American Golf Institute, ca. 1936.

_____. "Joy for the Average, Test for the Expert." *Sports Illustrated*, 6 April 1959, 38-43.

_____. "Learn How To Stroke The Ball." *American Golfer*, June 1931.

_____. *My Twelve Most Difficult Shots*. Minnesota: B&B, ca. 1929.

_____. "Not My Business." *Colliers*, 26 April 1930.

_____. *Rights and Wrongs of Golf*. New York: A. G. Spalding and Co., 1935.

_____. "St. Andrews Course Most Fascinating of All." *Atlanta Constitution*, 8 June 1927.

Jones, Robert Tyre Jr. and O. B. Keeler. *Down the Fairway*. New York: Minton Balch & Co., 1927.

_____. *How I Play Golf*. New York: American Sport Publishing Co., 1935.

Jones, R.T. Jr., W. D. Richardson, and Lincoln Werden. "The Ideal Golf Course." *Annual Golf Review Illustrated*, 1932.

"Jones Nears L.A. Enroute For Amateur." *Hearst Newspaper*, 20 August 1929.

"Jones Triumphs Again." *Outlook*, 7 September 1927, 6.

"Jones Wins Amateur Crown for Grand Slam." *Dallas Morning News*, 28 September 1930, 1.

"Jones Wins British Open Third Time." *Chicago Daily News*, 20 June 1930, 1.

Keeler, O. B. *The Autobiography of an Average Golfer*. New York: Greenberg Publishing, 1925.

_____. "Bob Jones Off to U.S. Amateur." *Atlanta Constitution*, 16 September 1930.

_____. "Bobby Jones Deserts Calamity Jane for 'Mike'." *Atlanta Journal*, 11 January 1931.

_____. "Bobby Jones' Golf Swing." *Atlanta Journal-Constitution Magazine*, 29 June 1947, 8-9.

_____. "Bobby Jones Wins National Open." *Outdoor South*, August 1923.

_____. *The Boy's Life of Bobby Jones*. New York: Harper & Brothers, 1931.

_____. "Gallery Gasps As Gunn Sinks 120-Foot Putt." *Atlanta Journal*, 3 June 1926.

_____. "The Grand Slam." *Golf*, September 1960, 31-33.

_____. "Golf Gossip." *Outdoor South*, March 1926.

_____. "Golf Gossip: The Director Gets An Idea for the Bobby Jones Movies." *American Golfer*, March 1931.

_____. "Jones and Adam Win Match." *Outdoor South*, September 1923.

_____. "Jones Writes More History." *The American Golfer*, August 1930.

_____. "Jones Tied Record to Lead Amateur Field." *Atlanta Constitution*, 24 September 1930, 19.

_____. "Looking at the South." *Golf Review Illustrated*, 1923, 37-38.

_____. "O. B. Finds Historic Sport Where Wallace Crawled to Die at Stirling Castle." *Atlanta Journal*, 30 May 1926.

_____. "Old England's Ideal Spot." *Atlanta Constitution*, 18 May 1976.

_____. "More than 100 Aces Made at East Lake: Jones Got Two." *Atlanta Constitution*, 20 September 1949.

_____. "The National Amateur Championship." *Outdoor South*, October 1925, 3-4, 22.

_____. "St. Andrews Course Most Fascinating of All." *Dundee Courier & Advertiser*, 10 October 1958.

_____. "Shoot The Works Says Stewart Maiden." *American Golfer*, 27 December 1924.

_____. "Today's Jones." *Golfing*, March 1941.

Keeler, O. B., and Grantland Rice. *The Bobby Jones Story*. Atlanta: Tupper & Love, 1953.

Kenny, H. F. "Secrets of the Master: The Best of Bobby Jones." *Choice*, July 1997, 1829.

Kertes, Stan, and Betty Hicks. "Hogan vs. Jones." *Golf Digest*, April 1955, 32-36.

Kindred, Dave. "Birthplace of a Legend." *Golf Magazine*, April 1994, 24-28.

_____. "Bobby Jones Made It So." *Sporting News*, 13 April 1998.

King, Augusta Wylie. "Golf as First Played in Atlanta." *Atlanta Historical Bulletin*, 8 (December 1947): 9-11.

Kinney, Bill, "Keeler and Bobby Jones." *Marietta Daily Journal*, 28 August 1975.

_____. "Keeler, The Story Teller, In Demand." *Marietta Daily Journal*, 29 August 1975.

Kirker, Thomas. "Pen Pals." *Golf Magazine*, April 1989, 80-85, 156-58.

Krout, John Allen. *Annals of American Sport*. New Haven: Yale University Press, 1929, 280-96.

Kupelian, Vartan. "Film Reflects Jones' Spirit." *Detroit News and Free Press*, 7 April 1996, 9.

_____. "Jones Biography Tops 95 Leaderboard." *Detroit News*, 21 November 1995, 2D.

Laney, Al. "He Does Not Live in the Past But in the Present of Golf." *Golf Digest*, March 1972.

Lieber, Jill. "Legend, Mentor, Friend: Celebrated Man Behind Masters is Lovingly Remembered." *USA Today*, 8 April 1997, 3C.

"Like Father, Like Fun." *Time*, 12 May 1941, 56-58.

Lonetree, Anthony. "Studies in Character." *Minneapolis Star Tribune*, 9 April 1996, 24A.

Longhurst, Henry. "Bobby in Britain." *Golf*, September 1960, 17-19, 51, 54, 55.

_____. "He Belongs To Us, Too." *Golf*, August 1965, 18, 60.

_____. "A Sad Loss." *London Sunday Times*, 19 December 1971.

"Loss to St. Andrews: Passing of Bobby Jones." *St. Andrews Citizen*, 20 December 1971.

Lowenberer, William, "Local Golf Veteran Remembers Bob Jones." *Baltimore Sun*, 19 December 1971.

Ludwick, Al. "Jones Started 1930 Streak in Augusta." *Augusta (Ga.) Chronicle Herald*, 2 April 1972, 4G.

McAndrew, Harry. "Why Bobby Jones Aimed to Hit the Crowd." *Glasgow Scottish Sunday Express*, 9 June 1957.

McCollister, Tom. "60 Years Ago Bobby Jones Made History." *Atlanta Constitution*, 27 September 1990, 1F.

McGill, Ralph. "Bobby Jones: Great Man and Great Golfer." *Atlanta Journal-Constitution Magazine*, 15 March 1953, 7-9.

MacKenzie, Alister. *The Spirit of St. Andrews*. Chelsea, Mich.: Sleeping Bear Press, 1995.

Maiden, Stewart. "A Lesson in Golf." *Outdoor South*, December 1923.

_____. "A Lesson in Golf: The Chip Shot." *Outdoor South*, September 1923, 10-11.

_____. "A Lesson in Golf: Putting." *Outdoor South*, August 1923, 15-38.

_____. "A Lesson in Golf: The Medium Pitch." *Outdoor South*, October 1923, 18-19.

_____. "Tips for the Round." *Outdoor South*, May 1925.

Martin, H. B. *Fifty Years of American Golf*. New York: Dodd, Mead, 1936.

"The Masters." *Sports Illustrated*, 6 April 1959.

"Masters Issue." *Golf World News Weekly*, 4 April 1972.

Matthew, Sidney L. " Along Came Jones." *The 1995 Masters Journal*, 6-9 April 1995, 120-27.

_____. "The Birth of Bobby's Dream Course." *Links,* April 1999, 54.

_____. "Bobby Jones' Calamity Janes I and II." *Golfiana 4* (1992): 3-11.

_____. *Bobby Jones Golf Tips*. Chelsea, Mich.: Sleeping Bear Press, 1999.

_____. "Bobby Jones' March on St. Andrews." *St. Andrews and Golf*. Cincinnati: Market Street Press, 1995.

_____. "Dreams Die Hard." *British Golf Monthly*, IPC Magazine, April 1998, 95-98.

_____. *Champions of East Lake— Bobby Jones and Friends*. Tallahasee, Fla.: I.Q. Press, 1999.

_____. "Essay on the Symmetrical and Balanced Theme." N.p.: privately printed, 1994.

_____. "First Pictorial History of Bobby Jones Original Hickories 1926-1930." *Golf Collectors' Society Bulletin*, November 1985.

_____. "Golf's Unsung Genius: Frank Sampson." *Centel Classic*. N.p.: Centel Corporation, 1989.

_____. "Impeccable Bobby Jones." *The Country Club*. Canaan, Conn.: Club Publications, Inc., 1996.

_____. "The Legacy of American Golf." *Fine Art of America's Fairways*. N.p.: Fine Art of the Fairway, Ltd., 1998.

_____. "The Life and Times of Bobby Jones." *Golf Magazine*, April 1996, 92-100.

_____. *The Life and Times of Bobby Jones*. Chelsea, Mich.: Sleeping Bear Press, 1995.

_____. "Luck or Destiny?" *1997 Andersen Consulting World Championship of Golf*. Largo, Fla.: ISM Group, Inc., 1997.

_____. *Secrets of the Master: The Best of Bobby Jones*. Chelsea, Mich.: Sleeping Bear Press, 1996.

_____. "Timeless Tips from A Legend." *The 1997 Masters Journal*, 7-13 April 1997, 118-21.

_____. "Who Stole Bobby Jones' Clubs?" *1996 Andersen Consulting World Championship of Golf*. Largo, Fla.: ISM Group, Inc., 1996.

"In Memory of Bobby Jones." *St. Andrews Citizen*, 8 August 1972.

"I Met A Man . . ." *Dundee Courier & Advertiser*, 13 October 1958.

McAndrew, Harry. "Why Bobby Jones Aimed to Hit the Crowd." *Glasgow Scottish Sunday Express*, 9 June 1957.

McGill, Ralph. "Bobby Jones: Great Man and Great Golfer." *Atlanta Journal-Constitution Magazine*, 15 March 1953, 7-9.

M'Finley, S. L. "Mr. Jones of Georgia." *The Glassford Herald*, 15 March 1952.

Middleton, Drew. "'Welcome Home Bobby,' Scots Cry." *Atlanta Constitution*, 4 October 1958, 10.

Miles, Ed. "Bonnie Bobby: Golfer of the Ages." *Southern Living*, April 1972.

_____. "Final Tribute Accorded Keeler by Sports World." *Atlanta Journal*, 16 October 1950.

_____. "Jones Completes Masterpiece." *Atlanta Journal-Constitution*, 18 September 1960, 8D.

_____. "Thirty Five Years Later." *Golf Digest*, August 1965, 50-51, 79-80.

Miller, Richard. *Triumphant Journey: The Saga of Bobby Jones and The Grand Slam of Golf*. New York: Holt, Rinehart & Winston, 1980.

Moon, Fred. "Big Bob Talks of Little Bob." *Atlanta Journal*, 3 August 1930.

"Mr. Bobby Jones' Great Golf." *The Scotsman*, 27 May 1930.

"Muffled Grief Pays Tribute to Way Bob Jones Lived." *Atlanta Journal*, 21 December 1971.

Murray, Jim. "A Major Success." *Golf Magazine*, April 1998, 24-37.

Neill, Nancy. *More than Bricks and Mortar: A History of the Atlanta Athletic Club*. Atlanta: W. H. Wolfe, 1987.

"The New Burgess of St. Andrews." *St. Andrews Citizen*, 11 October 1958.

"The New Golf Champion." *Outlook*, 29 September 1926, 137-38.

Newberry, Kevin. "Jones: Golf's Best Eternally an Amateur." *Houston Post*, 22 August 1993, 1B.

Nicklaus, Jack. *The Greatest Game of All: My Life In Golf, With Herbert Warren Wind*. New York: Simon & Schuster, 1969.

Nicklaus, Jack, with Ken Bowden. "Bob Jones Remembered." *Golf Magazine*, April 1995, 73-134.

_____. "My Favorite Lessons from Bobby Jones." *Golf Digest*, May 1989, 120-28.

"And Now Bobby Jones Plans to Golf for Pleasure." *The Literary Digest*, 11 October 1930.

"O. B. Keeler Tells Story of Fishing for Tarpon Here." *Sarasota (Fla.) Herald*, 1 August 1926.

"The Old Course at St. Andrews." *Strokesaver*. London: Ducam Mtg. UK Ltd., 1990.

"Open Golf Championship Bobby Jones' Great Triumph." *St. Andrews Citizen*, 23 July 1927.

"Open Golf Championship A Day of Thrills." *The Scotsman*, 24 June 1921.

"Open Championship." *The Scotsman*, 12 July 1927.

"Open Championship." *The Scotsman*, 13 July 1927.

"Open Golf Title: Mr. Jones Still Leads." *The Scotsman*, 13 July 1927.

Ouimet, Francis. *A Game of Golf: A Book of Reminiscences*. Boston: Houghton Mifflin, 1932.

Outlar, Jesse. "Amateur Made Atlanta Major Sports City." *Atlanta Constitution*, 28 September 1930, 1A.

_____. "A Simple Service." *Atlanta Constitution*, 21 December 1971.

"Packed Hall Sees Freedom Ceremony At St. Andrews." *Dundee Courier & Advertiser*, 10 October 1958.

"Par Wasn't Good Enough When Farrell Beat Bobby For the Open." *Literary Digest*, 7 July 1928, 52-56.

Parham, Betty. "Dixie Memories: Golf." *Atlanta Journal*, 10 March 1985, 3H.

Park, Hugh. "Great Golfer is Honored." *Atlanta Journal*, 12 November 1976, 23A.

Paxton, Harry, and Fred Russell. "A Visit With Bobby Jones." *Saturday Evening Post*, April 1958, 22f.

Peper, George. *Golf in America: The First One Hundred Years*. New York: Harry N. Abrams, Inc., 1994.

_____. *Grand Slam Golf*. New York: Harry N. Abrams, 1991.

_____. "Keeping up with Jones." *Golf Magazine*, August 1989, 8.

"The Perfect Amateur." *Outlook*, 21 July 1926, 399-400.

Perkerson, Medora. "How Bobby Will Make Movies." *Atlanta Journal*, 8 February 1931.

Perry, Ben. *Robert Tyre Jones: A Family Perspective*. Canton, Ga.: privately printed, 1990.

"Player of the Decade: Robert Tyre Jones Jr." *Golf Magazine*, January 1988, 48.

Pottinger, George. *Muirfield and the Honourable Company*. Edinburgh: Scottish Academic Press, 1972.

Powers, Francis J. "Bobby Jones Retires From Competitive Golf." *Golfers Magazine*, December 1930.

Pratt, J. Lowell, ed. *Sport, Sport, Sport*. New York: J. Lowell Pratt Company, 1963.

Price, Charles. *The American Golfer*. New York: Random House, 1964.

_____. "Bobby Jones Reveals His Inner Psychology." *Golf Digest*, August 1989, 40-41.

_____. "The Bobby Jones Training Films: A History and Perspective." *The Hickory Stick*. City: Callaway Golf USA, 1987.

_____. "The Champ." *Review*, March 1980, 24-31.

_____. "From Merion to Merion." *Golf*, September 1960, 14.

_____. *A Golf Story: Bobby Jones, Augusta National, and the Masters Tournament*. New York: Atheneum, 1986.

_____. "The Last Days of Bobby Jones." *Golf Digest*, April 1991, 184-88.

_____. "Robert Tyre 'Bobby' Jones: The Head Master 1902-1971." *Golf*, April 1972, 49-52.

_____. "Sir Walter and the Emperor Jones." *Golf Digest*, April 1992, 58-63.

_____. *The World of Golf*. New York: Random House, 1962.

Price, Charles, et. al. "The Bobby Jones Issue." *Golf*, September 1960.

Rabinowitz, Howard. "Bob Jones' First Retirement." *U.S.G.A. Golf Journal*, May 1993.

Rader, Benjamin G. *American Sports: From the Age of Folk Games to the Age of Televised Sports*. Upper Saddle River, N.J.: Prentice Hall, 1999.

Range, Willard. "P. J. Berckmans: Georgia Horticulturist" *Georgia Review* (Summer 1952): 219-26.

Rice, Grantland. "Bobby Jones on Golf." *Bell Syndicate*, 1930.

_____. *The Bobby Jones Story: From the Writings of O. B. Keeler*. Atlanta: Tupper and Love, 1953.

_____. "Interviewing Horton Smith." *American Golfer*, June 1930.

_____. "Jones An Artist." *New York Times*, 19 June 1926.

_____. "Scots Hailed Jones' Return." *Atlanta Journal-Constitution*, 19 December 1971.

_____. "Untrod Ground." *The American Golfer*, November 1930.

Richardson, William D. and Lincoln A. Werden. *The Golfer's Year Book*. New York: The Golfer's Year Book, 1931.

"Robert Tyre Jones (1902-1971): 'We Always Play the Ball as It Lies.'" *The Decorator's Show House*. Atlanta: Atlanta Symphony Orchestra, 1991, 18, 20.

Roberts, Charles. "Bobby Jones: Man, Legend." *Atlanta Journal-Constitution*, 19 December 1971, 1D, 10D.

_____. "Jones Ignored Weather in '33, Shot 67, Tops Until Bulla's 65." *Atlanta Journal-Constitution*, 8 February 1948, 14B.

Roberts, Clifford. *The Story of the Augusta National Golf Club*. New York: Doubleday and Co., 1976.

"R. T. Jones Double: Stirring Finish at Hoylake." *The London Times*, 21 June 1930.

Ruark, Robert C. "Atlanta's Bobby Jones Has Earned Immortality As A Great Sportsman." *Atlanta Constitution*, 21 September 1949.

Russell, Fred. "Bobby Jones' Favorite Masters Experience." *The Tennessean*, 9 April 1998, 2C.

Ryde, Peter. *Strokesaver: The Official Course Guide for the Old Course at St. Andrews*. Glasgow, Scotland: Stroke Sports Leisure Products/The Royal St. George's Golf Club, 1981.

"A Sad Loss." *London Sunday Times*, 19 December 1971.

The SAE Record, September 1926.

Salinger, H. G. "Jones Changes Mind About St. Andrews." *London Sunday Times*, 17 May 1930.

Salmond, J. B. *The Story of the R&A Being The History Of The First Two Hundred Years of The Royal and Ancient Golf Club of St. Andrews*. London: MacMillan, 1956.

Saporta, Maria. "Local Executives Honor Memory of Golf Legend." *Atlanta Journal-Constitution*, 2 June 1998, 3E.

Sarazen, Gene, with Herbert Warren Wind. *Thirty Years of Championship Golf: The Life and Times of Gene Sarazen*. New York: Prentice-Hall, 1950.

Schrock, Cliff. "Bobby Jones' Last Major." *Golf Digest*, April 1990, 113.

_____. "A Fellow Star Remembers Bobby Jones." *Golf Digest*, May 1991, 52-55.

Seelig, Pat. "Jones vs. Hagen." *Golf Magazine*, January 1993, 62-63.

Sheridan, James. *Sheridan of Sunningdale: My Fifty-Six Years As A Caddie Master*. London: Country Life, 1967.

Shiffman, Roger. "Classic Instruction." *Golf Digest*, June 1998, 52.

"Shots Out of Hell and Other Satanic Bunkers." *Golf World*, May 1994.

Sibley, John. "The Strength of Ethics." Reprint of the Robert Tyre Jones Jr. Memorial Lecture on Legal Ethics, Emory University Law School, Atlanta, Georgia, March 29, 1979.

Smith, Horton, and Dawson Taylor, with a foreword by Bobby Jones. *The Secret of Holing Putts*. New York: A. S. Barnes & Co., 1961.

Smith, Red. "Fore!" *American Heritage*, August 1980.

Sommers, Robert. "Bobby Jones: The Grand Slam." *Golf Magazine*, May 1995, 131.

_____. *Golf Anecdotes*. New York: Oxford Press, 1995.

"The Southern Gentleman." *Golf*, August 1965, 35-38, 57.

Spiker, Lawrence J. III. "A National Championship Comes to SAE." *The Record of Sigma Alpha Epsilon*, October 1923, 103-105.

"St. Andrews Greets Champ Bobby Jones." *Atlanta Constitution*, 4 October 1958.

Steel, Donald. "The Master." *Sunday Telegraph*, 19 December 1971.

Stiles, Maxwell. "Bobby Ready for Start of Film Career." *Los Angeles Times*, 2 March 1931.

_____. "Jones Arrives, Plays Lakeside." *Hearst Newspapers*, 22 August 1929.

Stump, Al. "History: Bobby and Ty." *Golf Magazine*, April 1990, 68-71, 91.

Symms, R. D. "Bobby Jones: Portrait of a Gentleman." *The Record of Sigma Alpha Epsilon*, Summer 1996, 4-7.

Tarde, Jerry. "Bobby Jones's Reputation Still Growing." *New York Times*, 9 April 1990, 55.

Taylor, Dawson. *The Masters: Golf's Most Prestigious Tradition*. New Jersey: A. S. Barnes, 1981.

_____. *St. Andrews: Cradle of Golf*. New Jersey: A. S. Barnes, 1976.

"Testing Different Putting Stances." *American Golfer*, June 1931.

"Thief Steals Bobby Jones' Prized Clubs." *Los Angeles Times*, 30 May 1929.

Thompson, Jimmy. "Yesterday's Golfers Were Better." *Golf*, April 1965, 18-20, 76, 78.

Thomy, Al. "Jones Returns to City Holding Fifth 'Freedom'." *Atlanta Constitution*. 15 October 1958, 31.

Tolhurst, Desmond. "A Most Beautiful Friendship." *Golf* (December 1993): 84-85.

Tolley, Cyril J. H. *The Modern Golfer*. New York: Alfred A. Knopf, 1924.

"Tommy Armour Analyzes the Jones Swing." *Golf*, August 1965, 25.

Townsend, James L. "Bobby Jones Is Dead." *Georgia*, January 1971, 11-12, 26.

Turbeville, R. T., ed. *Eminent Georgians*. Atlanta: Southern Society for Research and History, 1937.

"Tracking the 100 Greatest." *Golf Digest*, May 1995, 106-107.

Trevor, George. "A Little Flyer on Bobby." *Outlook and Independent*, 24 September 1930, 227.

"Triumph for Amateur Golf." *Dundee Courier & Advertiser*, 25 June 1921.

"25 Greats Pick Their Top Ten." *Golf Digest*, January 1996, 80-82.

"Unique Old Course Ceremony." *St. Andrews Citizen*, 16 September 1972.

Ward-Thomas, Pat. *The Royal and Ancient*. Edinburgh: Scottish Academic Press, 1980.

Wethered, Roger H. "My Impressions of Bobby Jones." *American Golfer*, January 1931.

Wethered, Roger and Joyce. *Golf From Two Sides*. London: Longmans, Green, 1922.

Weiskopf, Tom. "Leave it Alone." *Golf*, April 1998, 75-81.

Welch, J. Edmund. "Robert Tyre (Bobby) Jones, Jr., 1902-1971: His Victories Over Golf and Physical Affliction." Paper presented to the Annual Convention of the Midwest District, American Alliance for Health, Physical Education, Recreation, and Dance. Charleston, West Virginia. February 18, 1989.

"When Bobby Came Marching Home." *Mid-Week Pictorial*, July 1930, 6.

Wiggins, David K., ed. *Sport in America: From Wicked Amusement to National Obsession*. Champaign, Ill.: Human Kinetics, 1995.

"Will Bobby Jones Come Back?" *Outlook and Independent*, 11 February 1931, 43-48.

Williams, Joe. "Bob Jones Did Pros a Favor Quitting at 28." *New York World-Telegram And Sun*, 26 January 1960, 20.

Wind, Herbert Warren. "Anniversary at Winged Foot." *Sports Illustrated*, 18 October 1954.

_____. *The Complete Golfer*. New York: Simon & Schuster, 1954.

_____. *Following Through*. New York: Ticknor & Fields, 1985.

_____. "Mainly About Jones." *New Yorker*, 29 April 1972, 22, 126-28.

_____. *The Story of American Golf: Its Champions and Its Championships*. New York: Simon & Schuster, 1956.

_____. "Will Ye No' Come Back Again?" *Sports Illustrated*, 27 October 1958, 64.

Wright, Ben. "Surely the Greatest." *London Financial Times*, 20 December 1971.

Wright, David. "Sarasota Fetes Bobby." *The Record of Sigma Alpha Epsilon*, October 1926, 317.

Yun, Hunki. "Bobby Jones on Power." *Golf Digest*, February 1996, 89-92.